# THE INDEPENDENTS

## ANTOINETTE H. JONES

ILLUSTRATED BY

### TALITHA SHIPMAN

LD

The Independents
By Antoinette H. Jones

# CHAPTER ONE

"HEY SQUIRT, give me a hand, would you?" Matt called as he made his second trip down the hall towards the attic stairs. The muscles in his shoulders stretched under his t-shirt as he placed the two boxes on the floor next to the stairs. Matt grabbed one box and held the handle on the wooden stairs as he placed one box in the attic, then the other.

He was leaving today. He'd joined the Marines and had to go to the military base to start training.

Their dad was arriving soon to pick him up, and Chris was miserable. Chris just didn't want any more change in his life. First, their parents divorced and their dad moved out. Now, Matt was leaving, and tomorrow was the first day of school. He just couldn't catch a break.

He knew Matt was just putting his boxes in the attic, but to Chris it felt the same as when their dad put his boxes in the moving truck. Scary. Chris had lived his whole life with Matt there to guide and protect him. Now he would be on his own.

Matt was stepping off the last step by the time Chris made it to his bedroom door. Chris stood in the doorway, eagerly awaiting his assignment.

"Do me a fave," Matt said. "Will ya write my name on

those last few boxes in my room? I gotta get all this stuff put away before Dad gets here to take me to the airport." He grabbed Chris by the shoulder and pulled him into a side hug.

Chris cherished these moments. Matt had been so busy the last few weeks, they'd hardly had any time to hang out. Now Chris would be alone with their mom. Not that Chris didn't love his mom – he did, he just wasn't a fan of the way she'd been acting since their dad moved out. She was always saying, "I don't have to be what someone else expects me to be anymore. I'm free to be me!" Chris didn't understand what she meant. If she wasn't herself before, who was she? And who expected her to be different? He liked his mom the old way. The old her didn't interrupt him while he shot baskets in the driveway. The new her always wanted to talk and if Matt was gone, she would want to talk to Chris ALL THE TIME. Just the thought of it made his brain hurt. To Chris, his mom was like a giant girl and he had enough trouble talking to the regular size girls at school.

"Okay," Chris mumbled.

"Come on squirt. Cheer up. I'll be back before you know it," Matt said, smiling down at Chris.

"I'll know it," Chris said, lowering head.

"Come on," Matt said, guiding Chris to his room.

Matt walked into the room ahead of him and Chris stood frozen. He'd avoided looking in Matt's room all week, pretending nothing was going to change. Now he stood in the door looking at the bare walls, the made bed (Matt never made his bed), and the cardboard boxes filled with all Matt's things. He wanted to cry.

# CHAPTER TWO

"LET'S GO, Avery. You don't want to be late for your first day of school," Avery's mom called.

"Coming," Avery replied, as she slipped her feet into her shoes. Her mom was wrong though. Avery wouldn't mind being a little late for her first day of school. Maybe if she was late, she thought, she wouldn't have to walk into the building with the whole school. Maybe she could have a little quiet before she had to learn the lay of the land. Learning who was fun to hang out with, who was interested in the same things she was interested in, and who to avoid took time, and Avery wasn't really looking forward to it.

Avery liked to think of herself as what her mom called "an independent thinker." She liked the way that sounded. Her mom said that meant she could think for herself and didn't go along with the group when it didn't make sense. Avery agreed. Now she had to go to this new school and find other independent thinkers.

Avery wasn't really nervous. She had done this before - started a new school, but this time would be different. This time she was starting junior high school. Junior high school! That was only one school away from high school and two schools away from college. She'd seen a lot of the kids at the Kentland Junior High School Back to School Day last month. Some of them practically looked like adults!

She wasn't sure how this year was going to go, but she no longer felt like the top dog she'd been when she graduated from 6th grade. Now, she was back to the bottom of the ladder. And the worst part about it was she didn't know any of the players. At least if she'd gone to junior high school with her old friends, she would have had a crew to start with.

But no, her family moved out of the city and into the suburbs, so she could "stretch her mind." At least that's what her mom called it. Her mom didn't think that Avery's old school district offered enough diversity in the class schedule or the student body. Her dad just thought it was cool that she'd get to go to a school that had girls volleyball, basketball, track, and lacrosse. He was already planning their practice schedule, for whichever sport "piqued her interest."

No pressure.

As Avery's mom pulled into the carpool line, Avery could feel her stomach getting a little queasy. There were so many new faces. She watched kids getting off school buses, kids jumping out of cars, kids standing on the sidewalk and in the grass. Wasn't there a law about how many kids could attend one school? Finding friends was not going to be easy. The closer they got to the front of the line, the more Avery's stomach tried to send up the oatmeal her mom had made her eat for breakfast.

"Be cool," Avery mumbled.

"Huh? What'd you say, love?" her mom asked, as she quickly looked Avery's way. Her mom's hands squeezed the steering wheel a little, like they did whenever she was driving in traffic. Avery just knew her mom was worried about hitting one of the kids as they dashed through the cars to the school.

"Um, nothing," Avery said as she unknowingly placed her hand on her stomach.

She had to get it together. Rule number one at a new school - don't let 'em see you sweat.

# CHAPTER THREE

NATALIE COULDN'T BELIEVE her luck. She'd gotten Mrs. Thompson for Biology! Not that she was a fangirl or anything, but she was a fangirl. Mrs. Thompson had been on three episodes of *How Is That Science?*, Natalie's favorite television show! On the show, Mrs. Thompson gave demonstrations on how science was a part of everyday life. She'd shown how you could use bicarbonate of soda (aka baking soda) to remove pizza sauce from the carpet. With Natalie's two little sisters, Isla and Luna, always dropping or spilling things around the house, Natalie's stepmother had been very grateful to watch that episode with her.

If this was how her day was starting off, Natalie thought, maybe junior high school wasn't going to be so scary.

Natalie had been a little worried about starting junior high school. There were so many kids in this school that she didn't know. She felt small and everyone else seemed so big. At least most of the kids from her 6th grade class were at this school too, so there were a few familiar faces walking around and in the classroom.

Natalie wasn't great at making new friends. She was never quite sure how to start a conversation with someone she didn't know and she'd had a couple of bad experiences in elementary school. She knew that sometimes she could be too "mushy," or so her classmates had told her, but she cared about people and found it hard not to comfort them when they got hurt. She was also "too honest" sometimes and would say the first thing that came to her mind. THAT she learned could really be used against you in a friend group. So most of the time she stuck with the people she knew and trusted because that was where she felt safe.

However, this year, Natalie had decided she was going to put herself out there and "see what happens," as her dad had suggested. He told her that meeting people could be like a roller coaster ride – really scary sometimes, but after the scary parts, you'd walk around with a big smile on your face, so happy you wanted to do it again.


"Good morning class," Mrs. Thompson said. Her voice sounded musical to Natalie, but Natalie was a singer, so most things sounded musical to her. She heard music in her head all the time.

"Good morning, Mrs. Thompson," the class sang out.

"Welcome to Biology 101. My name is Mrs. Thompson and I will be your teacher."

Natalie was surprised Mrs. Thompson felt the need to make that statement. Everyone had to know who she was, Natalie thought as she looked around at her other classmates. The woman was famous, for goodness sakes. She couldn't believe there was anyone in the whole school who hadn't seen Mrs. Thompson on *How Is That Science?*

"Okay, let's get started," Mrs. Thompson said. She walked over to the wall and tapped the light switch. The classroom lights dimmed and music started to play.

Wait. Did everyone hear the music or was it just Natalie? That happened sometimes. She would hear music in her head that no one else could hear. Sometimes, it was like her brain was tuned into a radio station in another town. She would wake up and hear a song playing in her head, but it didn't match any of the songs playing on the little radio she had on her nightstand. It also seemed to Natalie that all important moments reminded her of a song or a melody. Natalie loved music and how it made her feel.

This time, however, she knew everyone could hear the music, because Mrs. Thompson started singing along, and the other students were laughing.

"Don't know much about history…" a man's voice was singing through the classroom speakers. Mrs. Thompson was singing along and walking between the desks, back to the front of the class.

"Does anyone know this song?" Mrs. Thompson asked.

Everyone started looking round at each other, seeing if anyone would be brave enough to speak up or knew the song. The song sounded familiar to Natalie. It was definitely older. Maybe it was something her abuelo had listened to when Natalie was little? But that was so long ago, she wasn't sure.

"Avery? How about you? Is this something you've listened to at your house?" Mrs. Thompson asked the girl sitting across from Natalie.

"No. I don't know this song," Avery said, looking around the classroom.

Mrs. Thompson looked a little sad and Natalie wanted to jump in to save the day, but she wasn't sure what to say.

"Well, that's okay. It's one of my favorites," Mrs. Thompson said. "It's a song called 'What A Wonderful World' sung by Sam Cooke. I fell in love with this song because it was the first time I heard one that combined two of my favorite things—learning and music! And that's what we are going to do in this class. We're going to share our love for science and enjoy a little bit of music." Mrs. Thompson's smile beamed out over the class and the students couldn't help but smile back.

Natalie felt like she was in a dream. It had to be a dream. Music and science in the same classroom—being taught by her favorite local celebrity! Natalie was not even sure what was said for the rest of the class. Her arms and hands moved on autopilot. She wrote words in her notebook and put papers in her folder, but she couldn't remember a thing after Mrs. Thompson said "science and music." Seventh grade was going to be the best year of her life, she thought as she walked out of the classroom.

# CHAPTER FOUR

SKYLAR STEPPED off the school bus and waved at Natalie. "See you Monday, Nat."

"Okay. Call me if you change your mind about going skating with us tomorrow," Natalie said, walking backwards in the opposite direction.

"I will," Skylar said.

But Skylar knew she wouldn't be able to go. She had to help her dad with the laundry tomorrow and make sure her little brother didn't break anything, when he was running around the house pretending to be Spiderman. Good thing he was cute or she'd probably tie the arms of his little Spiderman costume behind his back.

Since her mom had died, Skylar had to help her dad a lot more around the house. It was like he used all his energy at work every day and by the time he got home, he was too exhausted to do anything else. Skylar's mom had been great at taking care of them and doing everything around the house. Her dad used to say he and her mom were the dynamic duo. Then her mom would laugh and say that she was Batman. Her dad would smile, hug her mom and say,

"I'll be your Robin," while kissing her all over her face. Skylar used to smile at them and feel so warm inside. She could just feel the love flowing between them.

Those days were gone, but Skylar was glad she had the memories. Her mom always told her that when someone passed away, they were never truly gone if we kept their memories in our minds and their love in our hearts. Skylar kept both of those very close, so that she kept her mom with her always.

The first week of school had been great! Skylar and Nat were in PE together, so they didn't have to worry about being picked last for any team games and they always had a partner when it was time to pair up. All of her teachers seemed cool, and she had even figured out how much time she had to talk with her friends in between classes—or drop a note in someone's locker—and still make it to her next class on time.

There was also a new girl named Avery that seemed really cool. Skylar would have to pull her in and see if Avery and Nat liked each other. It would be awesome if they did.

Yeah, Skylar thought, she could handle junior high school. Life wasn't the same, but it was working out okay.

As she approached her house, Skylar's smile slid a little and she slowed her pace. "You got this," she repeated to herself.

Walking up the sidewalk, Skylar noticed the small changes that had taken place in the past year. Although her dad tried, he hadn't been able to keep up with yard work like he used to. The grass was a little too high, the bushes needed to be trimmed, and the flowers that her mom planted had weeds all around them. Even the numbers on the side of the mailbox looked like they were dropping a little.

The yard kinda looked like Skylar had felt since her mom died—a little forgotten. But now that school had started, Skylar felt a little lift in her spirits. She would be able to see her friends every day, and she had some things to look forward to.

The cool air hit her face as soon as she opened the front door. "Dad, I'm home," Skylar called. She really wished she could still say "Mom" instead.

# CHAPTER FIVE

"YOUR DAD SAID you're going to try out for the basketball team in a couple of weeks," Damien's mom said through the phone.

She tried to call every Friday night, but sometimes, depending where her Army unit was stationed, she didn't have phone service and Damien would have to wait weeks to hear her voice. His dad always made sure they ate dinner early enough on Fridays, so that if she called, Damien was free to talk.

"Yeah. Our PE teacher says I should," Damien replied.

"Well, that's great. That means he can already see your talent." Damien could hear the smile in his mom's voice. She LOVED basketball. When they all lived in the old house, the two of them would shoot hoops in the driveway all the time. Now that it was just him and his dad, he just played at school and on the basketball court next to the playground.

"Make sure you plant your feet and place your eyes where you want the ball to go," his mom instructed.

"Ma. I know. You taught me when I was five," Damien mock complained, but he really didn't care how many times his mom coached him on how to shoot; he was just happy to talk to her.

"I know, I know, but games are won or lost on the fundamentals."

"Ma."

"Okay, okay. Well, good luck. I'm cheering for you. How's school? Make any new friends?"

"School's good and yeah. This new family moved into the neighborhood and they have a daughter named Avery," Damien shared.

"Ohhh, Avery, huh?" his mom teased. "Is she nice?"

"Umm, I'm not sure. She seems cool, but we haven't talked that much. Do you know when you'll be home yet?"

There was a pause before his mom answered, and that made a knot form in Damien's stomach. "Well, it looks like the team is moving again, so probably not until December, but I'm praying to be home by Christmas," she said.

Damien's heart sank. His mom wouldn't be home for Thanksgiving. "That will be great. I miss you."

He knew not to say more. Damien was taught that the number one rule when someone was deployed was to not make them worry about home. If they were worried about home, they wouldn't have their mind on their job and they could get hurt. His grandparents told him that all the time when he was little. So, even though he wanted to tell his mom that he wished she didn't have to miss Thanksgiving and that he thought the Army should let moms come home for holidays, he didn't say it. He followed the number one rule.

"I miss you too, lil' man. Listen, I've got to go, but I love you and good luck with tryouts."

"Thanks, Ma. Love you too," Damien said, just before he heard the phone disconnect.

# CHAPTER SIX

OKAY, today was the day. Avery was going to eat lunch in the cafeteria. For the past few weeks, she'd been able to avoid going into the cafeteria, but she had no choice today. She could no longer hide in the library during lunch. Skylar had asked her to sit with her and Natalie, the girl from her Biology class, for lunch today. Avery couldn't say no to Skylar, one of the few African American girls in the whole school. Her mom might get some kind of "missed community connection" notification through her mommy sixth sense, and Avery would never hear the end of it. Her mom was ALL about her connecting with other African American kids in the community. She thought it would help Avery adjust to her new school. Little did her mom know, all African American kids didn't want to connect.

On the first day of school, there was an African American girl who had made it very clear that she wasn't interested in becoming friends with Avery. Avery had said hello to her—a girl named Jordan—when they sat next to each other in English. Jordan had given Avery a look of disgust that made Avery's neck snap back. Jordan had mumbled, "Hey" and quickly turned her head.

Whatever, Avery had thought. She may be new to this school, but she was not new to meanness.

"Over here," Skylar called, as she waved Avery over to a table near the end of the lunch line. Avery squeezed her tray a little tighter and walked over, making sure she didn't do something completely embarrassing, like trip and spill her food all over herself.

Can't let 'em see you sweat.

"Hey," Avery greeted, trying not to sound too excited to be out of the library.

"What up?" Skylar said, as she slid over a little on the bench seat to make room next to her for Avery to sit. "This my girl, Natalie. Nat, this is Avery."

"Hi," Natalie said with a warm smile from across the table. "We're in Biology together."

"Yeah," Avery said, nodding her head as she sat down.

Avery was immediately drawn to Natalie's eyes. They were dark brown and huge. They also shined like the smooth stones Avery's grandmother used to keep in a bowl by her bed. Avery had to force herself to look at something else, so she didn't come off as weird or something.

So she focused on Natalie's lunch. There were a bunch of brightly colored, square plastic containers, and each one had a different food or sauce in it. Compared to the school lunch Avery had purchased, and the peanut butter and jelly sandwich Skylar had in front of her, Natalie's lunch looked like it was made by a professional chef.

"Wow," Avery said, studying Natalie's containers. Had she said that out loud? Shoot! Her mouth had moved before her brain was able to catch up.

Natalie's cheeks got a little red and she smiled at Avery. "I know. Everybody says that."

"Yeah. Nat doesn't like for her food to touch," Skylar said, smiling at Natalie.

"Well, dang. I might have to get my mom to pay you to make my lunch, instead of me getting this stuff," Avery said, pointing to her tray.

They all laughed.

Yep, Skylar thought, Avery was cool.

They sat and talked all the way through lunch. Avery forgot about watching what she said or pretending that she wasn't bothered by anything. She enjoyed Skylar's funny comments and Natalie's easy laughter, and just relaxed for a bit.

# CHAPTER SEVEN

CHRIS WALKED INTO THE LIBRARY, hoping to hide. He knew he was being a coward, but he'd deal with his feelings about that later. Right now he just wanted to be by himself and he figured the library was a good place to go. Nobody went to the library during lunch time on Fridays—it was pizza day!

As he came through the door, Chris was startled to see Ms. Lupin standing at the desk. Didn't librarians eat lunch too?

"Well, hello Chris," Ms. Lupin greeted him.

"Umm, hi Ms. Lupin," Chris mumbled as he made his way to the table all the way in the corner, which was partially hidden by the last bookshelf.

Chris sighed in relief once he was in the chair. Riley had started bugging him again. He didn't know why, but it was happening. It was hard to understand what had happened between them. When they were little, they had been good friends. They hung out on the playground together, they were always at the same birthday parties, and they would even play catch after T-ball practice sometimes while Chris and his dad waited for Riley's dad to come pick him up.

But in 5th Grade, Riley started to change. He stopped

playing flag football during recess with Chris and the other guys. He started getting in trouble in class for talking back to Ms. Wilkerson. And he started being mean to Chris and some of the other kids.

At first, it was mean words. Somebody would make a joke about how hard the homework was and Riley would call them stupid or a baby. Chris mostly tried to ignore Riley back then, but he noticed the change in Riley's eyes and it scared him a little. Riley's eyes never seemed to get happy anymore, even when he smiled. When he smiled, it made Chris's heart beat faster and his arms feel cold.

The first time Riley hit Chris, it was a shock. "Hey! Why'd you do that?" he'd shouted at Riley, and had seen the smile that made him go cold. Riley hadn't answered. He'd walked away like nothing had happened.

After that, Riley became more aggressive. If they were playing a sport in PE he always pushed Chris too hard or threw the baseball, aiming it at Chris instead of at Chris's baseball glove. Chris did his best to avoid Riley, but they were in the same grade so sometimes it wasn't possible.

Then one day, it just stopped.

Chris was leaving school, walking across the big playground to go home, and saw Riley sitting on a swing. Riley's head was down and Chris was hoping that he could get by him without being noticed. He'd almost made it. Chris's heartbeat was slowing down and he thought he was home-free, but just as he was passing the monkey bars, Riley's head came up. When his eyes met Chris's eyes, they changed and he started to smile—the smile that made goosebumps come on Chris's arm. Riley jumped off the swing and headed straight for Chris. Chris decided he didn't want to wait to see what painful game Riley wanted to play, and started to run. He'd only moved a few steps before he hit something hard.

"Hey, bud. Where ya going?" Matt asked, smiling at Chris.

Chris stumbled back. Matt caught him by his shoulders before Chris lost his balance and fell on the ground. The relief of seeing his big brother almost took Chris's breath away. The relief must have shown on Chris's face because when Matt looked at Chris again, his smile faded. He looked over Chris's shoulder to see what Chris was running from.

"Hey, Riles. What's up," Matt asked, still looking from Chris to Riley.

"Nothing. Hey, Matt," Riley replied.

Chris noticed that Riley's voice sounded the way it used to when they were real friends, and Matt would babysit them while their parents went out together.

"Where are you guys headed?" Matt questioned.

"Nowhere," Chris responded quickly. "What are you doing here?"

"Mom forgot that you have a dentist appointment today and asked me to come get you. We need to get home." Still looking from Chris to Riley, Matt continued, "Why don't you tag along Riles? I know your folks aren't home yet and it's been forever since you've been over for dinner."

"Umm," Riley hesitated.

"Aww, come on," Matt said, putting one arm around Riley and the other around Chris, as he guided them down the path to their home. "My mom will call and let your mom know you're with us."

For the rest of the day, it was like they were friends again. Matt made a joke about the squirrels playing in the street, holding up traffic, and Riley actually laughed. Not his creepy laugh, but a real laugh—and he kept laughing and joking at the dentist's office, on the ride back home, and through dinner. Chris didn't have to wonder what had happened. It was the same thing that happened his whole life—Matt happened. Chris didn't know how he did it, but Matt always knew how to make it better and everybody loved him. So, Chris didn't have to wonder why Riley's personality suddenly became better, he already knew the answer—no one could resist his brother. Without him even having to go to his brother for help, Matt had fixed the problem.

After that day, Riley hadn't bothered Chris. They didn't become friends again; it was more like Riley forgot about Chris, which Chris knew wasn't possible, but as long as he didn't have to worry about what Riley would do next, he didn't care.

Now, Riley remembered Chris again. It started with little things again, but Chris knew it was only a matter of time before he'd have to start looking over his shoulder again. So, Chris's first idea was to sit in the library during lunch. Riley didn't like Ms. Lupin. He said she was nosy and always minding other people's business, so he avoided her like homework during a holiday break.

Chris knew this wasn't a long-term solution. Maybe he should tell his mom or dad? He should have told Matt before he left, but Chris was in junior high school now—he wasn't a little kid and he couldn't keep running to his big brother all the time. No, he could handle this without Matt. His dad had told Chris that when Matt left for the military, Chris would be the man of the house. Chris did not feel qualified to be the man of the house, but he definitely wasn't going to be a baby either.

Chris looked around at the books on the shelves. Next time he came to the library for lunch he would have to plan ahead and put one of his comic books in his bag. For now, he'd see what was on the shelf.

As he scanned, he saw that one book looked different from the rest. He got up and pulled it off the shelf. It was a composition notebook with "Bio" written on the front. Ugh! Chris thought. Whoever wrote this book was never going to get kids to buy it. No one would want a book that looked like homework! Curious as to what would cause someone to write a book about biology, Chris flipped it open.

It wasn't a library book—that was good to know. It was someone's class notes.

Score! Chris wanted to pump his fist in the air! Biology was not easy for him and maybe whoever's notes these were had written down something that he could use. Chris sat at the table and started reading. Maybe there was something in here about meiosis. Chris just didn't get it. Why were cells just dividing and having babies all willy nilly?

Once he got to page four, the writing changed. What Chris was reading was no longer about biology, but someone's life. "I can't believe we're moving," it read. "I have lived my whole life here. My friends are here. I don't know anyone who lives out there."

Chris read on.

Whose book was this? He looked back at the beginning of the book, then flipped to the back. No name. Chris was just about to go back to read some more, when someone touched his shoulder.

"Huh?" Chris jumped.

"I said, you'd better start packing up. The first bell has already rung," Ms. Lupin said.

"Oh, okay." Chris gathered the composition notebook and put it in his backpack. Ms. Lupin started walking back to the front of the library. "I'm happy to see you using some time to study," she said over her shoulder. "Let me know if you want to join our biology tutoring group. We meet here on Tuesdays after school. It's free."

"Thanks. Uh, maybe," Chris said as he hurried through the door. Knowing he had the notebook in his backpack made him feel like his steps were a little lighter. He couldn't wait to get home and read more.

# CHAPTER EIGHT

DAMIEN SAT ON HIS BIKE, one leg on the ground and the other balancing on a pedal, staring at the sunset. It had been a long day and he was glad to have time to just ride his bike. He wasn't sure why he liked this time of day, but there was something about watching the colors of the sky change that always made him stop and look. He didn't stop for long, though; the street lights were coming on and if he wasn't home his dad would worry.

Damien didn't want his dad to worry. It was just the two of them now. Damien got back on the path and headed home.

"Dad! I'm home," Damien called as he walked into the house. Well, not quite a house. They used to live in a house on the other side of the development. Damien would sometimes ride his bike by there, just to see if anyone was sleeping in his old room. Now, since his parents split up, Damien's dad said they didn't need all that house, so they moved into the condos.

"In the kitchen," Damien's dad shouted.

"Coming."

"Wash your hands," his dad said, and Damien was glad his dad couldn't see his face when he rolled his eyes.

As they sat down to eat, Damien looked at his dad and wondered if he should ask about Thanksgiving. His dad had never been a big talker (his mom said he was the strong, silent type, but he was always thinking), but since his parents separated his dad talked even less. Damien had to study his dad's movements to see what kind of mood he was in.

"Thanks for dinner, dad," Damien said, as he bit into his Sloppy Joe sandwich. The saucy ground beef started sliding out the opposite side of the bun with his first bite. His dad always put too much of the Sloppy Joe mixture on the bun and Damien loved it!

"You're welcome, son," his dad said, looking up from his plate and focusing on Damien.

Okay. Now was a good time.

"Mom said she probably wouldn't be home for Thanksgiving."

The slight rise in his dad's eyebrows was the only movement Damien saw on his dad's face for almost a full minute. Then his dad slowly blinked his eyes and took a deep breath.

"Oh, yeah," his dad said solemnly.

"Yeah," Damien said, swallowing his bite of food. He waited patiently for his father to say more.

"Well."

Damien stared at his dad, willing him to say more. C'mon, Damien thought, say more.

"I guess we'll visit your grandparents for Thanksgiving. You can take the Polaroid and send your mom some pictures afterwards," his dad said.

Damien let out the breath he was holding. Okay, that was a plan. He wasn't sure which grandparents yet, but that didn't matter. As long as it wouldn't be the two of them sitting at this table, like they did every night for dinner, Damien would take it. Damien loved his dad and he knew that his dad loved him, but without his mom or even the buzz of being on an Army base around them, it was just too quiet.

His parents had said their separation was for the best, but Damien couldn't tell who it was best for. Neither of his parents seemed as happy as they used to be and he certainly didn't like it. Now he had to have these awkward conversations and it always seemed like he was playing a game of Post Office between his parents because they barely spoke to each other. So who benefited from this new arrangement? No one that he could see.

"Do you think we will be able to talk to her?"

"I'm not sure, but if she gets a chance to call, I'm sure she will," Damien's dad said.

"It's gonna be weird," Damien said softly, still looking at his dad.

"It'll be different, that's all," his dad said has he got up from the table, taking his plate.

"You didn't eat your food."

Damien's dad looked down at his plate and back at Damien.

"I'm not really hungry. I have some reading to do."

His dad scraped all the food on his plate into the kitchen trash can and put his plate in the sink. Once he rinsed his plate and fork, he walked over and stood next to Damien.

Damien looked up, as his father placed his hand on Damien's shoulder and gently squeezed.

"Finish up your dinner and get ready for bed. I'll come check on you shortly," his dad said. One side of his dad's face lifted in an attempt to smile, but it was like the other side of his face couldn't get up enough energy to do it too.

"But," Damien said, wanting to protest the end of their conversation. He had more questions. Were his parents actually getting a divorce? Since they moved out of their old house, where was his mom going to live when she came home from deployment? Was his dad going to call his grandparents and let them know about Thanksgiving? He had questions.

"Don't worry," his dad said as he walked down the hall to his bedroom.

Don't worry, Damien thought, how was he supposed to do that? His mom would know. His mom would have sat at the table and they would have made the Thanksgiving plans all together. His dad would have nodded his head at whatever his mom decided and said, "That sounds good, Candice." But now his mom was FAR away, and Damien had no one willing to answer his questions.

# CHAPTER NINE

AVERY TORE up her room looking for her journal. She wanted to write down her thoughts before she forgot anything that happened in school this week. She moved blankets and comforters, emptied her backpack and went through all the books on her shelf. She even crawled under her bed and pulled out EVERYTHING. Where could it be? Calm down, she told herself. If you panic, you'll miss it.

So she tried to keep her cool while she looked, but it was getting harder to do so. To Avery, this was not just any journal. No, this was her super personal journal. The place she wrote all her thoughts and feelings. Where she didn't have to pretend she wasn't scared—even when she was. Where she wrote down all her hopes and dreams. Where she wrote things that would be embarrassing for someone else to read! Ugh! Where could it be?

Wait! Avery stopped and stood in the middle of her messy bedroom. Maybe it fell out in her mom's car? She had tossed her backpack into the backseat of the SUV on the ride home today. Avery turned and ran out her bedroom door.

She rushed down the stairs and through the kitchen.

"No running," her mom shouted from the spare bedroom she used for her office.

"Yes, ma'am," Avery said as she almost crashed into the door leading to the garage.

She opened the back door of her mom's SUV and climbed inside. She didn't see anything but her mom's big umbrella, with the curved handle that Avery liked to hold in the rain because it was gigantic and kept her whole body dry.

Avery knelt on the floor of the backseat and slid her whole arm under the passenger seat. Nothing but some loose change and a couple of old french fries. She crawled across to the other side and did the same thing under the driver's seat. No journal.

Avery took a deep breath and climbed out of the car.

Now what? It wasn't in her mom's car. It wasn't in her room. It was nowhere. Avery had looked everywhere and still she couldn't find her journal. She tried to remember the last time she had it. The last time she remembered writing was a couple of days ago during lunch—IN THE LIBRARY.

That's where it must be. Okay, okay! It must be in the library. As soon as she got to school in the morning, she was going to the library. She would have to hurry, so that she wasn't late getting to class, but nothing was more important than getting her journal back.

# CHAPTER TEN

"I DON'T KNOW where else it could be," Avery almost whined into the phone.

"Ms. Lupin said she didn't see it?" Skylar asked from the other end of the phone line.

"She said she's seen lots of biology notebooks, but nobody turned one in and she hasn't found one."

"Do you think someone picked it up?"

"I'm gonna be sick," Avery said, placing her hand on her stomach. "You really think somebody has my journal?"

"It makes sense. You've looked everywhere and no one else has seen it. It's too big to fall in the corner and nobody sees it," Skylar said matter-a-factly.

"Ugh," Avery sighed. Her eyes were beginning to well up and tears threatened to roll down her cheeks.

"Don't worry. I think we can find it. Can you meet at the basketball court? I'm going to ask my boy Damien to help us and it'll be easier for us to talk without any adults around," Skylar offered, hoping to comfort Avery. She wasn't exactly sure how they were going to find Avery's journal, but she knew that if anybody could help, it would be Damien. At least she hoped he could.

"I guess. If we find out somebody has my journal..." Avery said, with a warning in her voice.

"It's the only thing that makes sense. But don't sweat it. We'll find it," Skylar said with her typical optimism.

"Okay. Let me get my shoes on and I'll meet you at the court," Avery agreed. Her tears had dried and she was feeling the fuel of her anger. If someone had her journal, there was going to be a problem.

# CHAPTER ELEVEN

"DAD. I'm going to ride my bike. I promise to be back by dinner," Avery said as she walked to the door of her dad's home office. He was sitting behind his wooden desk in the chair Avery's mom tried to get him to throw away when they moved. The chair was black with a silver pinstripe pattern, like a suit or ugly tie. Avery remembered how much she loved to sit in that chair when the cushions were full and fluffy, but now it had permanent dents from her dad's butt and the cushions no longer fluffed when he stood up. Her mom said it was time for a new chair. Her dad said he didn't have time to break in a new chair, especially since this one already fit him perfectly.

Avery's dad looked up from his computer and stared at Avery, arching one eyebrow. The jazz music playing in the background reminded her of her grandfather. Pop-Pop loved listening to jazz. He said the saxophone spoke words not written in the English language.

"Dad. MAY I go ride my bike, if I promise to be back by dinner?" Avery knew what that look meant and changed her earlier statement into a question. Her dad did not believe children should tell adults what they were going to do. Children were to ask permission.

"That sounds better. And where is this bike ride taking you?" her dad asked. Although his voice was stern, the twinkle in his brown eyes always made Avery feel that his face could break into a smile at any moment.

"I'm just going to the playground by the lake, to meet my friend from school."

"And what's this friend's name?"

It took all Avery's control not to roll her eyes. When they lived in the city, she never got all these questions. She would ride her bike through the neighborhood, to her cousin's house, to see her grandparents, even to the store—and her dad didn't care. Now, he clocked her every move and it was annoying. He knew she could handle herself. What was the big deal? Weren't the suburbs supposed to be safe?

"Skylar," Avery said with the least amount of attitude she could muster.

"Okay. Have fun and be safe. What time is dinner, Avery?" her dad asked, even though he knew the answer. It was his way of making sure Avery knew what time he expected her home.

"6:30," Avery said, with her phony smile and tilting her head to the side. All the braids in her ponytail went to the side too, tickling her ear a little.

"Mmmm hmmm," her dad said, nodding his head and going back to whatever he'd been doing on his computer.

Once she was sure her father couldn't see her face, Avery turned and rolled her eyes. She loved her dad, but when he treated her like a baby, he really got on her nerves.

Avery walked out the front door and picked her bike up off the grass. She thought about going back inside for her jacket, in case it got chilly later, but didn't want to chance another conversation with her dad. It was only the beginning of fall; she should be fine. She really needed to focus on finding her journal. Skylar sounded hopeful that they would find it. Avery hoped they would, and soon, before anyone read her private thoughts. That would be so embarrassing!


Chris was rolling his dirt bike from the backyard as his new neighbor rode by him on her bike. What was her name again —Amber? Chris couldn't remember. He was going to wave, but she went by pretty fast and didn't even turn her head his way. He hadn't built up the nerve to talk to her yet, but thought he could start with a wave.

Chris had been so excited when she moved in next door, because there hadn't been a new kid on their street in years. Unfortunately, his mom had already decided that the new family next door was "not their kind of people." Chris wasn't sure what that meant, but whenever his mom said it, he knew she wasn't inviting them over for dinner. Some of the ladies in the neighborhood had formed a book club and they would take turns going to each others' houses. Then, in the summer, it would be backyard barbecues, and people's whole families would go.

But if his mom said a family was "not their kind of people," Chris never saw the mom at book club, and the family never attended a backyard barbecue. When Chris's dad lived with them, he always said, "people are people," but his mom would say, "oil and water don't mix."

Was Chris oil or was he water? What about his mom, his dad, and Matt? He wasn't sure and his mom didn't explain. As far as Chris felt, he'd rather be chocolate - everybody loved chocolate.

# CHAPTER TWELVE

DAMIEN WAS DRIBBLING the basketball on the half-court beside the playground when Skylar and Natalie rolled up on their bikes. It wasn't big enough for a full-court game and it only had one hoop, but the boys still played on it all summer long, while they waited to get back inside the gym at the start of each school year.

"Hey, Day," Skylar called out, as she dropped the kick-stand on her bike and stood in the mulch at the end of the court. Her pink and white matching sweat suit made it look like she was ready to play basketball, but the shiny white sneakers she was wearing showed no sign of ever being used for sports. Damien knew Skylar would not risk messing up the polish on her nails to dribble a basketball.

"What up?" Damien replied as he shot the ball, and it sailed into the hoop.

Natalie smiled at Damien, but couldn't get her voice to work. That always happened around Damien. Her brain would freeze and she couldn't remember words. She put her bike next to Skylar's and walked to stand next to her.

"What's the mission?" Damien asked as he dribbled over to where the girls were standing.

"Helping out my girl," Skylar replied. "Her journal is missing and I think somebody took it."

Just as Damien opened his mouth to reply, Avery skidded into the mulch and stopped two inches from Natalie. She put her feet down, stood with her bike between her legs, and leaned on the handlebars.

"Hey Nat and Sky," Avery said. Then she turned and gave Damien a long head to toe look.

Damien looked at Avery and raised his eyebrows. What was her problem?

"Hey Avery. This is my boy Damien I was telling you about," Skylar said, noting Avery's look at Damien. "Day's cool. You don't have to worry, he knows how to keep a secret and he's got a real way of getting people to open up to him. I think he can help." Skylar walked over to Damien and put an arm around him to show her support. He was a bit taller than Skylar, so her arm landed on his elbow instead of his shoulder.

Before anyone could speak, Chris slowly rolled up the walking path and into the mulch, but didn't join the group. He stopped his bike a few feet away. Chris could feel some tension coming from the group and wasn't sure what to do. Damien had asked him to meet him at the court, so Chris wasn't sure what the girls were doing here. They couldn't be here to play basketball - Skylar Robinson did not play basketball. She got her dad to write her a note to get her excused from even playing basketball in PE.

"Heeyy, Chris!" Damien called, walking away from the girls towards Chris.

"What is he doing here?" Avery whispered to Skylar.

"I don't know," Skylar replied, lifting her shoulders. "I didn't invite him."

The girls focused their attention on Damien and Chris.

"Aye. Y'all know Chris, right?" Damien asked the girls, as he pulled Chris closer to where the girls were standing.

"Umm, yeah," the girls replied.

"Well, since Sky said we had a mission, I told Chris to come help. He's really good with figuring out puzzles. Last year, he helped get us out of a puzzle room, way before the time was up," Damien beamed.

Chris shrugged. "I watch a lot of detective shows. What's the mission?"

All eyes turned to Skylar, who turned and looked at Avery for permission to share with Chris.

"Okay, he's good with puzzles, but can he keep a secret? I don't need everybody at school to know my business," Avery said, looking directly at Chris.

Chris swallowed.

"Yeah, he can keep a secret," Damien said, while putting his arm on Chris's shoulder and leaning into him. "He knows my biggest secret and hasn't told anybody - since 5th grade!"

Chris beamed at the praise and stuck his chest out a little.

Again, Skylar looked at Avery, waiting to see if she should continue.

Avery rolled her eyes at the boys and turned to Skylar. "Do you trust them?"

"I trust Damien and if he says Chris is cool, I believe him. Plus, I know a Damien secret too and I know he wouldn't want me to share either," Skylar said, pursing her lips and tilting her head at Damien.

"Why you gotta go there, Sky?" Damien asked, throwing his hands up in the air. "ANYWAY, we came to help y'all. If y'all don't want our help, we can go."

All eyes turned to Avery.

Avery was unsure of what to do. This was when she really missed her friends from her old neighborhood. There, she knew everybody. She knew not to tell Kurambi ANYTHING she did not want the whole neighborhood to know, cause that boy spread news like a reporter on TV. And she knew she could trust her friend Toya with her life, but she didn't REALLY know any of these people. Skylar and Natalie had been cool and she didn't think that they might be fake. She'd seen Damien in school and he was always nice enough, but she wasn't sure about Chris. He lived next door and would smile sometimes, but he never spoke and his mom was definitely fake.

Everyone waited for Avery's answer. Damien was ready to stick up for Chris, if Avery didn't believe Chris could be trusted. Skylar was trying to think of other people who might be able to help them find the journal, if Avery didn't want Damien's help. But she was really hoping Avery would say yes, because it was hard to find people who knew how to keep a secret.

"Okay, fine. But this is top secret. If you say a word to ANYONE - ANYONE, you will be sorry," Avery said, narrowing her eyes and pointing to Chris.

Chris stepped forward to defend himself, but Damien spoke before he could say anything.

"Dang girl, relax. I said he was cool. Now, will somebody tell us the plan, before we have to get back home? I still need to study for Mrs. Thompson's biology test."

"Ugh," everybody groaned in unison. They all liked Mrs. Thompson's biology class, but her tests were killer.

"Well," Skylar spoke up, taking one last look at Avery before she continued, "here's what happened. Avery had her journal with her when she went to the school library, but when she got home and took her stuff out of her backpack, it wasn't there."

"So, I went back to the library yesterday," Avery added, "and looked everywhere, but I couldn't find it."

"Did you ask Ms. Lupin? Maybe she found it," Damien said.

"Of course," Avery said, rolling her eyes and blowing a puff of air from her mouth. If this was what Damien was going to ask, she didn't think he was going to be much help.

"Okay," Damien said, "just asking."

"I asked if she'd seen my biology notebook, but she said she hadn't," Avery added.

"I thought we were looking for your journal," Natalie asked.

"We are," Avery said. "I disguise my journal to look like my biology notebook, so if anyone finds it, they won't know what it is right away." Avery smiled as she revealed her secret.

Chris froze. It couldn't be the same book. His heart started to beat a little faster as he listened.

"That's genius," Natalie exclaimed. "I would never have thought of that."

"Thanks," Avery said. "I learned it from my cousin. Her mom is a big snoop and always going into her stuff, so to keep her out of her business, she's got to be smart."

"Are you sure you didn't leave it anywhere else?" Damien asked.

"I looked everywhere. My backpack, my locker, my room, everywhere. I know somebody has it," Avery said, narrowing her eyes as if she could picture the face of the person with her journal.

Chris's heart was beating so loudly now, he was surprised that no one else could hear it. How could the book he found belong to Avery? The person he wanted to get to know was his next door neighbor. Was this a joke?

"What about Mrs. Thompson? Maybe somebody gave it to her, since it said 'biology' on the front," Natalie asked.

"Yeah," Skylar said. "What about her?"

Avery looked hopeful. "I didn't ask her. I was too busy looking everywhere else, but I guess." She hunched her shoulders.

"Okay. So step one is ask Mrs. Thompson. If she doesn't have it, we have to go on a search. Who do you think might have it?" Damien asked.

"I don't know. Maybe one of the Jordans," Avery suggested, mentioning two girls who were very popular at school and known for being in everybody's business. Both their names were Jordan and they'd been best friends since kindergarten. They spent so much time together, people just called them "The Jordans," like some weird music group.

Chris opened his mouth to say something. He wouldn't want the wrong person to be accused, but Natalie spoke first.

"I don't think so," Natalie said.

"Yeah, if one of them had it - you would know. They would tell the whole school what you wrote," Skylar added.

"Or use it to torture you," Damien said, nodding his head.

"Then I don't know," Avery said, lowering her head in defeat. "Y'all know these people better than me. Who do you think would take it?"

"Is anyone mad at you right now?" Damien asked.

"Or acting funny, like they know something?" Skylar added.

Chris blinked. Was he acting funny right now? Was everyone looking at him?

"I don't know," Avery said. She was trying to think about the people she had met at school, but no one came to mind.

"I think we should all pay attention at school tomorrow. We can see if anyone is acting weird or being mean to Avery," Natalie suggested.

Okay, Chris thought. They didn't think it was him.

"That sounds good," Damien said. "We can do some recon, meet back here tomorrow after school and talk about what we saw."

Skylar scrunched up her face. "What's recon?"

"It's from the military. It means watching and paying attention to people and stuff," Damien answered.

"Oh, okay. That sounds good. Whatcha think, Avery?" Skylar asked.

"I guess. I don't see what else we could do," Avery responded.

Chris opened his mouth again, but no sound came out. Would Avery hate him for reading her journal? She seemed so upset about it. He didn't read much, but what he did read made him think they could be friends. Having a new friend right now - especially one that lived next door – would be more fun than sitting in the house looking at Matt's empty room. Maybe he could find a way to drop the journal at her house without her knowing it was him?

"Well, I gotta go. If I'm late my dad will worry," Damien said walking away from the group.

"Allright. We'll meet back here tomorrow," Skylar said walking towards her bike. "Ready, Nat?"

"Um, yeah," Natalie replied. "Don't worry Avery. I'm sure we will find your journal."

Since they weren't good friends yet, Natalie had to put her hands in her pockets to keep from hugging Avery. In her family, everybody hugged to comfort each other, but she didn't think Avery would want a hug in front of everybody.

"Thanks," Avery said as she watched Natalie and Skylar

walk to their bikes. She turned her bike towards the path and started walking.

Chris was standing on the path, holding the handlebars of his bike.

"You okay, Puzzle Boy?" Avery asked.

Chris blinked and looked at Avery, "Uh?"

"I said are you okay? You haven't said anything in a minute."

"Oh, yeah. I was just listening." He turned to face Avery. "Why'd you call me Puzzle Boy?"

"Cause you said you were good at puzzles," Avery said, tilting her head and placing a hand on her hip.

"I am," Chris said defensively.

"Well I hope your skills will help me find my journal - and soon. I hate the thought of someone reading my stuff." Avery made it up to the path and was about to start peddling when she noticed Chris still hadn't moved. "You coming?"

"Huh," Chris asked. He was having trouble getting his mind to work. There were so many thoughts going through his head at one time.

"I said, are you coming?" Avery rolled her eyes and shook her head. How was this boy going to help her find anything? He couldn't even keep up with the conversation.

"Are we riding together?" Chris asked with a little too much hope in his voice.

"We might as well. We live next door to each other."

Chris lowered his head a little, too nervous to say what was on his mind. "Um, yeah. Cool."

Avery and Chris started riding towards their houses. They were both thinking about Avery's journal. Avery was worried that someone was reading all her private thoughts, but the idea that Mrs. Thompson might have it gave her a little hope. She was going to hold on to that little bit of hope or else she might start crying right now, and there was no way she would embarrass herself by crying in front of Chris.

Chris, on the other hand, was thinking that he had to tell Avery that he knew where her journal was, but the words just wouldn't come out. He would find a way to get her journal back to her without her ever knowing he'd had it, and everything would be okay. He wished Matt was home.

# CHAPTER THIRTEEN

AS AVERY and Chris rode up the sidewalk, Avery expected Chris to stop at his house, but he kept riding until they reached hers.

"You passed your house," Avery said, once they stopped in front of her garage. The door on the right side was up, so she could see her mom's car. She didn't know what they were having for dinner, but the rumbling in her stomach reminded her that it must be almost dinnertime.

"Yeah, I know," Chris said. He stopped on the sidewalk, but didn't ride up into Avery's driveway. The weight of what he should say felt heavy. He wanted to tell Avery that he knew where her journal was, but then he would have to explain everything, and he didn't want to look weak to Avery. And he didn't want her to hate him for reading her journal.

Avery waited for Chris to say more. He looked like he wanted to say something, but he was just standing there. "Okay, then…"

"I never noticed that your house was the same as mine, just switched," Chris blurted out, looking at both of the houses. Avery's house had their two-car garage on the left side and Chris's house had their two-car garage on the right side, but other than that they were built exactly the same. They were both painted cream with brown doors, even, but Chris's mom had filled their front yard with flowers, and Avery's house only had green bushes.

"I'm sure you didn't," Avery said. "You're usually moving pretty fast when you go by my house."

Chris could pretend that he didn't know what Avery was talking about, but he already felt too guilty about the journal. "Sorry."

"What did you say?" Avery said softly.

"I said, I'm sorry. I wanted to say hi when you first moved in, but I was scared. Sorry," Chris said, looking at Avery with such sad eyes, Avery felt like she should apologize to him.

"Why were you scared to say hi?" Avery asked.

"I don't know," Chris said, looking at his house, then back at Avery.

Avery followed his eyes and looked at his house. She didn't see anything.

"Well, no need to be scared of me Puzzle Boy - unless you tell my business," Avery said, trying to make a joke.

Chris smiled. "Yeah, I heard."

"Best you remember," Avery said as she walked her bike into the garage. "I gotta get inside, but I'll see you tomorrow."

"Okay, yeah. See you tomorrow."

Avery put her bike next to her dad's bike on the rack and headed into the house through the side door. She peeked to see if Chris was still standing on the sidewalk, but he was already gone. She was still wondering why Chris would be afraid of her, when she closed the door.

"I'm home," she yelled once inside.

"Wash your hands," her mom yelled back.

Avery was happy to. The smell of fried chicken made her stomach grumble louder.

# CHAPTER FOURTEEN

AFTER FINISHING HIS DINNER, Damien got up from the table and did the dishes. That was their routine now. His dad cooked and Damien did the dishes. "We're a team," his dad would say. "We share the work, so no man gets too worn down." That sounded right to Damien. He could pull his weight. Right now, however, he wished they were a team of three again. Damien wanted to talk to his mom about helping Avery.

Damien's mom always knew what to do. She was good with helping Damien organize his thoughts and strategize, as she called it. She said Damien had the makings of a good leader; he was good at thinking for himself and not blindly following what other people said, he was considerate of others, and he planned out how he was going to reach his objective. Those things, his mom said, were what good leaders were made of. Well, what Damien could use right now, was his partner. But she wasn't here, so he would try with his dad.

"Dad," Damien said as he sat on the couch next to his

father. The football game was playing on the television and Damien knew his dad would be really into the game, but he didn't have any other choice.

"Yeah?" his dad responded, without looking away from the game.

Damien took a deep breath. "One of my friends needs help."

"Is anyone hurt?" His dad asked, looking towards Damien with concern in his eyes.

"No. Nobody's hurt," Damien said, shaking head.

"Oh, okay," his dad said as he turned back towards the television and relaxed against the couch cushion.

"She's not hurt, but needs my help finding something," Damien said. He had to make sure he didn't give away too many details that would get his dad worried and cause him to call anybody's parents. Skylar would run him over with her bike, if that happened. And he didn't know Avery very well, but she was definitely high strung. He'd rather not have to explain to her why all of their parents were asking questions. She made it very clear that she wanted as few people to know about her journal as possible.

"Well, you're good at helping and finding stuff. I'm sure you two will figure it out."

"Yeah. I was thinking maybe we could strategize, like me and mom used to."

"That sounds great, Damien. I knew you had a plan," his dad said, never taking his eyes off the television.

"But, I meant..." Damien started, but his dad interrupted him.

"Hey. Why don't you call him, while I finish watching this game?" his dad said, patting Damien on his knee, dismissing him.

"Okay. Even though it's a her and not a him," Damien mumbled, as he moved from the couch and walked down the hall to his bedroom. What would his mom have said, Damien thought? She would probably have said, start from the end and work your way backwards. Okay, he thought. Let's give this a try.

# CHAPTER FIFTEEN

SKYLAR WALKED into her house and paused, listening for sounds of her little brother and dad. She didn't hear anything, so she let go of the breath she'd been holding and closed the front door. Not that she didn't want to see her dad and little brother - she loved her family, but she had a lot on her mind right now and if her little brother DJ were around, she wouldn't be able to concentrate on the current problem. She had to help Avery find her journal.

Skylar frowned as she walked to the stairs. The thought of someone reading her diary scared her. Her heart started to beat a little faster just thinking about it. If Skylar were Avery, she thought, she'd be freaking out right now. Fear made Skylar move quickly up the stairs and into her bedroom to make sure her diary was still in its hiding place.

Skylar entered her sunlit room and quickly closed the door. She passed by all the stuffed animals on her bed, went into her closet and opened her purple shoe box. Skylar kept the box at the very bottom of the stack of shoe boxes on the left side of her closet. Inside, on top of her diary was the last pair of shoes she and her mom bought together - three weeks before her mom went into the hospital and never came home.

The box that held a pair of shoes that she could no longer wear, because they were two sizes too small, but that Skylar just couldn't throw away. Inside the diary were Skylar's deepest, most private secrets. She wrote in her diary about missing her mom, being scared sometimes, and her dreams for the future. She would just die if anyone read it!

But there it was, right where she'd left it. All purple and glittery, with her name spelled out in rhinestones. Still holding all her secrets and dreams. Still private.

"Sky!" she heard her dad calling her from downstairs.

"I'm in my room," she called back, looking at her bedroom door to make sure it was still closed.

"Come give me a hand, would you? I gotta bring the groceries in and DJ needs to go potty."

"Coming," Skylar said as she placed her diary back in the shoe box and shoved the box back to the bottom of the stack.

Skylar bounced down the stairs, her small gold hoop earrings swaying back and forth in her ears as she came to her little brother at the bottom of the stairs. He was doing the pee-pee dance and trying to get the strap loose on his denim overalls. Her dad, Derrick senior, must have gone back out to the car, because she didn't see him anywhere.

"Come here. Let me help you," Skylar said to Derrick junior, as she reached for his denim strap.

"Sky," DJ said cheerfully. The relief in his big brown eyes warmed Skylar's heart. She helped him into the half-bath near the garage door, so she could also hear her father if he needed help.

"Finished," DJ chimed, as he pulled up his underwear and overalls.

"Wash your hands," Skylar demanded, as she turned on the water to make sure it wasn't too hot or cold for his little hands.

"I didn't toush anything," DJ said. He still struggled to pronounce the "ch" sound when he spoke. Skylar thought it was so cute, but knew he would get teased if he didn't get better with the "ch" sound by the time he finished kindergarten in June. Sometimes kids could be mean.

"You'd better wash your hands, little man. Bubbles on the front and back," Skylar said, as she flipped her hands to show him what she meant by front and back. DJ clipped his last overall strap and bent down to put his bright red step stool in front of the bathroom sink. Skylar left him in the bathroom and went to check on her dad.

Derrick senior still hadn't come back inside the house, so Skylar went into the garage. When she opened the door, her dad was sitting on an old grey folding chair, holding something in his hand.

"Daddy," Skylar said quietly.

He looked up at her, with the same big brown eyes as DJ, and a sad smile. "How has it been in the trunk all this time and I've never noticed it?" He was looking down at the small, black stick in his hand.

Skylar walked over to him to get a closer look. "What is it?"

"It's Tish's," her dad mumbled, looking down, keeping the small smile on his face. LaTisha Renee Robinson, Derrick Robinson's one true love, and Skylar and DJ's mom.

Skylar moved closer to him and asked quietly again, "Daddy, what is it?"

Derrick grabbed one end and pulled off a smooth black cover. Then, he turned the handle back and forth, revealing bright yellow and white colors between the black flaps. Next, he pushed a button on the handle and the umbrella popped open. The bright yellow and white colors formed a sunflower pattern on the small umbrella.

"Sunflowers, her favorite," Skylar said, as she watched the bright pattern turn in her father's hands.

"Yeah," Derrick said, looking down at the opened umbrella.

"I wash my hands, Sky. Bubbles front and back," DJ yelled from the open side door. He turned his hands back and forth, mimicking the same motion Sky showed him in the bathroom. "Can I have a snack?"

"Yes. One sec," Skylar said and turned back to her dad. "Daddy. Do you need help bringing in the groceries?"

Her dad did not respond.

Skylar's heart started to beat a little faster. "Daddy," she said again and touched his arm. His skin was warm against her hand and she could feel the muscles moving underneath, as he continued to turn the umbrella.

Her dad looked up, but his eyes did not meet hers. "Um, no. No thanks, princess. I'll be in, in a second," he said, but continued to look down at the umbrella, turning it back and forth.

Skylar looked around, but there was no one there but DJ. What should she do? Should she push or leave him here? Grandma Tooshie said that sometimes you just had to give him a moment to work his way through things. And Grandma Tooshie was dad's mom, so she should know best, but Skylar didn't tell Grandma Tooshie that sometimes that moment took days.

Skylar decided not to push. Instead she walked to the side door and bent down to be face to face with DJ, who was waiting patiently.

"What chu want for snack Lil' Man?" she asked DJ, and put her hand on his shoulder.

"Jello," he cheered, showing all his teeth.

"Nah. Nice try, but jello is not a snack."

"Uh hun," DJ said nodding his head. "Jace had a jello cup for snack at school today." He argued, very proud of himself for providing evidence to his sister in defense of his snack choice.

"Well, at 1627 Willow Bark Drive, jello is dessert. How

about some carrots?" Skylar responded, using their full address to bring home her point.

"But," DJ interjected, looking around as if another piece of evidence of jello being a snack was somewhere nearby.

"But nothing. Applesauce with cinnamon is my final offer," Skylar said, standing up straight, putting her hands on her hips.

"Okay," he mumbled, letting out a big huff, his cheeks drooped and his bottom lip poked out.

That softened Skylar's stance and she reached out to grab his face with both her hands and kissed his forehead. "Come on Mr. Pouty. If you eat all your vegetables at dinner tonight, we'll have jello for dessert."

DJ's face brightened and he turned to go inside the house and find the applesauce.

Skylar turned back to look at her father. He was still twirling the umbrella in his hand, looking at nothing in particular. Skylar didn't think he noticed her and DJ, and if he did, it didn't cause him to react. She looked at him for another second, but the sound of DJ opening the kitchen cabinet made her feet move to go inside. If her dad was not inside by the time she finished giving DJ his snack, she'd come back out and get him.

# CHAPTER SIXTEEN

LATER THAT NIGHT, Chris lay in his bed, unable to sleep. He felt bad for taking Avery's notebook from the library. He didn't know it was hers when he took it, but he'd known it belonged to someone. He could have taken the notebook to Ms. Lupin, but he didn't. It had been so nice to read that someone felt some of the things that he felt, he'd just wanted to read more. That notebook had made him feel a little less lonely, and not miss Matt and his dad so much. With both of them gone, the house was just so quiet. Matt wasn't playing his music or talking on the phone. His dad wasn't watching TV or making noise in the basement. And his mom had a part-time job now, so even she wasn't there as much to ask him questions about his day or yell at him to pick up his stuff.

When he read the notebook, Chris thought that maybe he would find who it belonged to and he could make a new friend. In his imagination, Chris thought that he would find the person, give them back their notebook and they would be so grateful, they would try to do something nice for him - to show their gratitude. Then, Chris would say, he was glad to return it, and maybe then the owner of the notebook would invite Chris over to their house after school, and Chris would have a new friend. Now he had to find a way to get the notebook back to Avery.

# CHAPTER SEVENTEEN

THE NEXT MORNING, Chris was walking to school early. He'd told his mom that there was a morning study group in the library, so she wouldn't ask too many questions when she noticed him leaving the house earlier than usual. It wasn't a complete lie. Chris was headed to the library. He'd thought about it all night and decided that this was the best way to make sure Avery got her journal back, without her finding out that he'd read it. It was simple. He would just put it back on the shelf where he found it. Then he would go back to the library during lunch, pretend to find it again, and give it to Ms. Lupin. Simple.

As Chris walked through the gate behind the school, he saw him - Riley. Chris knew this day was coming. His heart was beating fast as he tried to walk quickly across the grass field. What should he do? How could he avoid this situation? He quickly looked left, then right, hoping to find someone or something to draw Riley's attention away from him. But he only saw green grass and the sidewalk leading to the school. Anyone who was there was inside the school or around front. Was there something he could say? He knew he couldn't outrun Riley, so he didn't even try. Chris just put his head down and kept walking. Why couldn't Riley just leave him alone!

These were the times he missed Matt the most. His older brother always knew what to do and always protected him. Before their parents got divorced, Matt was always the one to comfort Chris when their parents would argue. When he was little, if Chris got scared in the middle of the night, he would go into Matt's bedroom, instead of downstairs to their parents' room - which seemed way too far when there might be a monster in the house. Matt never made Chris feel embarrassed about being scared. If it was a really bad night, Matt would even sleep on the floor next to Chris's bed and be on guard, in case the monster came back.

But Matt wasn't here and Riley was getting closer.

"Hey, Chris," Riley called. "Where you going?"

"I gotta get to the library," Chris said, walking a little faster. He didn't turn around to look at Riley, so he didn't see it coming when Riley grabbed his backpack and pulled it off his shoulders.

"Why you in such a hurry?" Riley asked, holding Chris's backpack out of reach. He had that scary smile on his face, and he pushed Chris's hand away when Chris reached for his backpack.

"Give it back Riley," Chris demanded. "I told you I have to get to the library. I don't have time to play."

"Then go. I'm not stopping you," Riley laughed.

"Come on. Stop playing around."

"Who's playing? I'm just getting my backpack from you," Riley said, giving Chris the smile that reminded him of a creepy clown.

"That's not your backpack, Riley, and you know it," Chris pleaded.

"Really? It looks like mine," he said, not even looking at the backpack. "How do I know you didn't take it out of my locker?" Riley said as he started walking backwards, away from Chris.

"It was not in your locker, Riley. Come on!" Chris was getting desperate. Riley was getting farther away and no one was around to help. Chris started moving towards Riley. He had to get his bag back, but he didn't know what to do.

"Well, I gotta go. See ya, Chris," Riley sang as he turned and started to jog away from Chris.

"Give it back," Chris said, reaching for his backpack again. When he grabbed one of the shoulder straps, it caused Riley's body to jerk back a little. That must have surprised Riley because he almost let the backpack go, but when it was almost off of his arm, he turned around. And he was no longer smiling.

Riley stopped moving and used both his hands to push Chris hard. Chris fell down in the grass, shocked by the force of Riley's push. For a second, Chris thought Riley was surprised too, but it was too fast. Within a blink of his eye Chris saw the creepy smile return to Riley's face. "See ya tomorrow Chris," he said as he walked backwards away from Chris. Before Chris could even get up off the ground, Riley turned, ran onto the path and out of sight.

# CHAPTER EIGHTEEN

AT LUNCHTIME, Natalie and Skylar sat at their usual table, waiting for Avery. They had both taken their assignment for the day very seriously. They watched and listened to everyone in each of their classes, to see if there were any signs or whispers of anyone knowing about Avery's journal.

"Okay. I wrote down the names of everybody I saw acting weird today," Natalie announced as she pulled out a piece of notebook paper.

"Dang! Your list was so long you had to write it down," Skylar said, as her eyebrows moved so high on her forehead, they almost touched her hairline.

Natalie laughed at the expression on Skylar's face. "No! I just thought it would be more scientific if we wrote down all of the names, so we could keep track."

"Girl. Why you gotta make everything scientific? I swear…" Skylar said shaking her head and smiling at Natalie.

"You'll be glad when we gather all the information and compare."

"When we what?"

"Hey," Avery said, as she sat across from Natalie and Skylar at the table.

"Any luck with Mrs. Thompson?" Skylar asked enthusiastically.

Avery made a sad face and shook her head, no.

"Sorry," Natalie said, wishing she could go around the table and give Avery a hug.

"That's a'ight. We gonna find it - soon," Skylar said, looking at Avery.

"Yeah, and when we do, somebody is going to be really sorry," Avery said, between her teeth. She was holding her jaw so tight that the air from her saying her 's' made a little whistling sound from between her teeth.

"We'll meet Day and Chris after school and see if they know anything," Skylar said.

"Yeah, we'll find it," Natalie added. "Did you notice anyone acting weird today?"

"No more weird than usual," Avery said. "No one said anything mean or acted like they knew a secret or something about me. Did y'all notice anything?"

"I didn't, but we still have two more periods," Skylar said, trying to sound hopeful.

"I only noticed Oliver Kang acting weird today. Did anyone else notice him? He kept going to his locker and looking around like he was hiding something in it," Natalie added.

"Oh, that wasn't about Avery," Skylar said, laughing. "That boy was trying to sneak a mouse out of school from his Life Sciences class. I think he said it was cruel to keep it in the cage or something."

"Really? That's what he was doing?" Natalie asked, smiling.

"Yeah," Skylar said, with a bright smile, "Principal Williams took him to the office right before lunch."

"Well, that's just great," Avery said, placing her chin in her hand and putting her arm on the table. "We're right back where we started."

"Sorry," Natalie said, losing her smile.

"Well, Nat. I guess we won't need to make a list," Skylar said, sadly.

# CHAPTER NINETEEN

"WHAT DID YOU SAY?" Avery said, as she slammed her bike into the mulch and started marching towards Chris. Her light brown eyes were bright with anger and shooting daggers his way.

"Whoa, hold up," Damien yelled, standing in front of Chris with his hands splayed out, to hold Avery back. He was blocking Avery's view of the person who'd betrayed her. She tried to move her head around Damien's shoulders to look at Chris's face.

They had come together for their planned meeting after school. No one saw any kids acting suspicious at school today or being weird towards Avery (except for Oliver Kang, his mouse rescue was the talk of the 7th grade). They were beginning to start planning on what to do tomorrow, when Chris blurted out his secret - he knew where the journal was and who had it.

Chris looked down at his shoes. His sandy blonde hair fell forward and covered his entire forehead, but not before Avery saw the sadness in his eyes. But she couldn't care about that right now. He had betrayed her. She thought that they could be friends, but friends didn't lie to each other.

She tried to go around Damien again to get to Chris. Chris didn't back away or try to hide from Avery's anger. He stood there.

"I said I know where it is, or at least who has it, and where I think it is," Chris said in a low voice.

"Then why didn't you tell us yesterday?" Avery yelled. She was barely holding back her angry tears. She hadn't been able to get much sleep last night and couldn't concentrate in school today. She kept thinking about someone reading her journal and knowing her deepest secrets.

"I…I was going to. I tried to, but…" Chris stuttered.

"But what?" Avery yelled. She was so angry, her whole body was vibrating. Damien was using a lot of strength to hold her back from Chris. "No one was stopping you. All you had to do was say, 'Hey Avery, I have your journal.'"

"I…I don't have it. Not anymore. I'm sorry," Chris said, raising his head and looking Avery in the eyes. The honesty she saw in those blue eyes made her stop trying to get past Damien.

Chris hadn't slept much last night either. His dad always told him, "Let your conscience lead you and you can't go wrong." Until yesterday, Chris didn't exactly understand what that meant, but his mind kept telling him that it was wrong to let someone else get in trouble for taking Avery's journal, when he was the one who took it from the library. And he thought that his plan to return the journal would make everything all right, but Riley had blown that plan to pieces. So, once he gave up on trying to find Riley before school, he made sure to sit next Damien in their 1st Period Art class and tell him what had happened. Damien had been a little upset with Chris for not telling him yesterday, but he was more upset that Riley had been picking on him and had taken his backpack.

Skylar and Natalie both gasped.

"Chris," Natalie whispered.

"Why didn't you tell us?" Skylar asked. At least she didn't look as angry as Avery. Chris saw the confusion on her face and wanted to run away.

"I wanted to. I really did, but I...I couldn't," Chris pleaded.

"So WHERE is it?" Avery said, holding her arms at her sides with her hands balled into fists.

You could hear the leaves on the trees blowing in the wind, as everyone waited for Chris's answer.

"I think it's at Riley's," Chris said.

Avery's neck jerked her head back like it had been actually pushed by Chris's words. Her eyebrows folded in and her nose scrunched in confusion. "Who?" she said, confused.

"Riley," Skylar asked.

"How did he get it?" Natalie asked.

Chris felt like the questions were coming so fast he didn't know which one to answer first.

"Aye. Slow down. Give my boy a sec and he'll explain," Damien said, as if he could read Chris's mind.

Skylar stepped from behind Avery and looked surprisingly at Damien, "You knew?"

"What? Wait, no," Damien defended himself, because he knew that he did not want three angry girls to start yelling at him. He could handle one at a time and stand up for Chris, but if all three turned on them - he and Chris might have to make a run for it. "Chris just told me today. Just give him time to explain."

Chris took a deep breath and told them everything – well, almost everything. He was too embarrassed to tell them that reading the first few pages of Avery's journal had been the first time he felt like he wasn't alone, in a long time. He couldn't tell Avery that reading her thoughts had comforted him and made him miss Matt a little less. He didn't know how to express the hope he had when reading her words that he and Avery could be friends for real. So he told them everything else. He told them how he found the journal in the library, but didn't know who it belonged to. He told them how he had it in his backpack, and how Riley had taken his backpack while the journal was still inside. He also told them that BECAUSE Riley had his backpack, he'd missed turning in three homework assignments and if the teachers called his mom he was toast!

"Okay, okay," Avery said, as she began pacing in the mulch. "This isn't bad. It's not a big deal. Only one person has seen my journal…maybe two." She was talking out loud, but not to anyone in particular.

"Well, tell Riley to give it back," Skylar demanded.

"Yeah, or we will tell his parents," Natalie added.

"You think I didn't tell him to give it back?" Chris asked. His voice was getting louder. He was starting to feel the anger he felt at Riley for taking his backpack. "I ran to his house after he took it, to get it back, but when I got there his house was empty. His family doesn't live there anymore. I don't know where he lives and he wasn't in school today." Chris was moving his hands around so much while he was talking, that at one point Natalie thought he was going to hit himself in the face.

"Uuuggghhh," Avery groaned. "I just want my journal back." She stopped pacing and plopped down in the mulch. Her whole body seems to sag, like she didn't have the energy to hold it up anymore.

"We'll get it back," Natalie said, crouching down next to Avery.

"Yeah, I already thought of a plan to find out where he lives," Damien added, bending over and placing his hand on Avery's shoulder.

Natalie saw his hand on Avery's shoulder, and how close his face was to her face, and her brain short circuited. Her cheeks felt warm and she couldn't remember the words she was about to say.

"Well, let's hear it," Skylar said excitingly, sparing Natalie from being embarrassed by her reaction. "I knew there was a reason I called you in on this mission!"

"See, Riley rides bus #22, with my boy Tre'. So I'll ask Tre' to ask his parents if I can come over tomorrow after school and hang out. I'll ride the bus home with Tre' and see where Riley gets off," Damien said.

"But what if he doesn't come to school tomorrow?" Avery asked.

"Then," Damien continued, "I was thinking that maybe Natalie could check the Parent Teacher Association addresses, since her stepmom is president of the PTA."

Everybody looked hopefully at Natalie.

"Um," Natalie said. Her big brown eyes seemed to grow with the deep breath she took.

"Come on Nat. You can do it," Skylar encouraged. "Do you know where she keeps her PTA stuff?"

"Uh huh," Natalie said, nodding her head. "But I'm not allowed to go into the office without permission. She and my dad said that room is for working, not playing."

"Then get permission," Avery said. She was starting to feel better. Having a plan meant this whole nightmare could be over soon. They knew where the journal was, and all they had to do was get it from Riley.

"How?" Natalie asked.

"Ask permission to go into the office for something else," Avery said. Natalie thought she could actually see Avery's mind thinking behind her eyes, as Avery was coming up with the idea of how to get the address. "Then, while you're in there, get the address from the PTA list."

"I don't know," Natalie said, looking doubtful. Although Rachel was not her birth mom, she was a great stepmom and Natalie did not like the idea of lying to her.

"Please, please, please, Natalie," Avery said, grabbing Natalie's hand. "I know we're not real friends yet, but I really need your help. I promise, I will owe you big if you can get that address for me."

Natalie turned and saw the hope in Skylar and Damien's eyes, and could not say no to the pleading in Avery's eyes. No, she and Avery weren't best friends or anything, but she liked Avery - and she wanted them to become real friends. So, Natalie slowly nodded her head, hoping the brown curtain caused by her long hair was hiding the fear on her face. She wanted to be a good friend and a good daughter at the same time.

# CHAPTER TWENTY

NATALIE PLACED her hand on the cool doorknob of her parents' office and froze. Did the metal from the door handle just cause her heart to stop beating for a second? Did she get an electrical shock from the doorknob? No, no, she told herself, she had already learned about electricity. You needed friction for an electrical shock. Besides, she didn't feel anything but scared right now, and she didn't need electricity for that. No, no, she was holding her breath. That was what was causing that pain in her chest. Shaking her head, Natalie blew out a big breath and tried to calm herself. "You can do this," she whispered to herself as she opened the door.

Avery had pleaded with Natalie to look for the address tonight, instead of waiting until tomorrow. She said she was too afraid that Riley would read her journal or worse - lose it, and they would have to go through this all over again. So, Natalie had agreed to start the plan when she got home from the basketball court.

Natalie had asked Rachel if she could borrow the stapler from the home office. Simple. Rachel said yes, but to make sure her little sisters Isla and Luna did not follow her into the office, because the office was not for playing. So here Natalie was, going through the door of her parents' office, while her heart was beating a hundred miles a minute - or at least that's how it felt to her.

She walked into the room and looked at the two small desks. It was easy to tell which desk belonged to her dad and which desk belonged to Rachel. Her dad's brown desk was really just a strong wooden table with lots of paper stacked on one side, a phone in the middle, and a green cup with lots of pens inside. Behind it was a large, black office chair that spun around, and a huge black filing cabinet that was taller than Natalie. Directly across from her dad's desk was Rachel's desk. Natalie thought Rachel's desk was so pretty. It was an old fashioned wooden desk that Rachel had bought from a yard sale and painted a bright blue color (like number 36 in the crayon box of 96). Her desk only had a few pieces of paper, neatly stacked at the top, a small vase that held a couple of daisies, and a lamp with a multi-colored shade. Rachel's desk had a soft white chair that didn't spin, but had arms that swirled and were attached to the seat with another piece of wood.

Natalie looked back at the door and took a deep breath. Here I go, she thought. She walked over to Rachel's desk. She stood still to listen and make sure she didn't hear any noise in the hall, although she couldn't hear much over the beating of her own heart in her ears. Natalie pulled opened the top drawer of the desk and found the stapler right where Rachel said it would be. She placed the stapler on top of the desk and turned around to look at the short gray filing cabinet behind the desk. Unlike the huge filing cabinet behind her dad's desk, this filing cabinet only had two drawers. Natalie knew Rachel kept the PTA stuff in one of the drawers, but wasn't sure which one. She slowly pulled open the first drawer, trying to be as quiet as possible.

There were lots of files in the drawer. *Dios mío*, Natalie thought. How was she ever going to find the right folder?

She looked at the labels on the folders. They were in alphabetical order! Yes! She just had to look for a folder starting with the letter "P" and she could get outta here. Natalie started moving through the folders: "Dentist," "Homeowner's Insurance," but she didn't see a folder label that started with the letter "P."

Natalie gently closed the top drawer and grabbed the handle for the bottom drawer.

"Did you find it?" Rachel said as she walked into the office.

Natalie's head whipped to the side as she faced the door. Her hand was still on the drawer handle. Her mouth dropped open and her eyes got as big as saucers.

Rachel didn't move. She looked at Natalie with confusion. "What's going on, Natalie?"

Natalie lowered her head, letting her hair fall forward to hide her face and the shame she felt.

"Natalie," Rachel said.

Natalie stood up and turned her body towards Rachel, but she didn't say anything.

"What's going on?" Rachel asked, as she slowly turned and closed the office door.

"I'm sorry," Natalie said, once she could use her voice.

"Sorry for what, mija? What are you doing?"

"I...I..." Natalie stumbled over her words as she looked back and forth between Rachel and the filing cabinet. She was trying to think of something to say, but her mind was blank. She couldn't think of a way to get Riley's address and not get into trouble.

Rachel walked across the room and put her hand on Natalie's shoulder. "Talk to me, mija. Tell me what's going on."

Hearing Rachel use the term of endearment just made Natalie feel worse. Rachel was always so loving and kind to Natalie. Natalie didn't want to lie to Rachel, but she also didn't want to go back and tell Avery and Skylar that she couldn't get Riley's address. Natalie began to cry.

"Oh, Natalie," Rachel pleaded and she pulled Natalie into her arms, hugging her and stroking her hair. "Why are you crying? Please tell me what's wrong."

And Natalie did. She told Rachel everything. She told Rachel about Avery's journal, and Chris keeping it a secret, and Riley taking it, and them trying to get it back because Avery was so worried that someone was reading all her private thoughts. Rachel just listened, the way Rachel always listened when Natalie needed to talk. She sat in her white desk chair and waited for Natalie to finish spilling everything and stop crying.

"Wow. You kids have been busy," Rachel said, looking sympathetically at Natalie.

"I'm sorry I lied about why I wanted to come into the office," Natalie said, eyes looking at Rachel pleading for forgiveness. "I just wanted to help. I feel so bad for Avery."

"Is Avery your friend?" Rachel asked.

"Well, not yet, but you and Papa always say it's good to help people in need. And even though we're not real friends yet, I like Avery and she's nice to me, and I want to help her get her journal back," Natalie said, barely taking time to breath in between sentences.

"You're right," Rachel agreed. "We do say that and it's a good thing that you guys want to help, but I am not happy about the lying."

"I know. Sorry," Natalie said, lowering her head and looking at the carpeted floor. "I didn't want to lie, but they said we weren't telling our parents because parents can't be trusted to keep secrets." Natalie raised her head and looked Rachel in the eye again. "But…"

"Yes, mija. You and I have always been able to keep our secrets," Rachel said, taking both of Natalie's hands into her hands and squeezing gently. "And you know I will help you, as long as I know you are safe. You have to promise me that you will not put yourself in any danger, and that if you need help you will come to me."

"I promise," Natalie exclaimed as she threw her arms around Rachel's neck.

"Okay, okay," Rachel said with a soft laugh, hugging Natalie back. "I know you are a smart girl and I believe you can think for yourself - even when you really want to help someone. So, I'm going to give you this family's address." She pulled a folder from the bottom drawer of the file cabinet. Natalie was so relieved, she didn't have time to appreciate that the alphabetical order of the files continued into the second drawer. "But, if you feel like things are getting out of hand or you need an adult - you come and tell me, immedi-atamente."

Natalie nodded her head, as Rachel wrote the address for Riley's house on a piece of note paper she pulled from the top drawer of her desk.

"Promise me," Rachel demanded, holding the paper out to Natalie. "Your Papa will be angry with both of us if you get hurt and he knows I helped you."

"I promise," Natalie said. "Papa will never know. I do not want him to worry."

"Okay. Here ya go," Rachel said handing the note paper to Natalie. Natalie gently took the paper from Rachel. Rachel took her hands and placed them on both sides of Natalie's face and looked Natalie in her eyes. "You are very special to me too and I would worry if something happened to you."

Natalie had to blink her eyes a few times to keep from crying. "I know," she whispered. "I will be careful."

"Good," Rachel said with a smile, as she lowered her

hands. "Now you and your friends go and get Avery's journal back."

"Thank you, thank you, thank you," Natalie said, giving Rachel one last hug before she darted out of the office and headed towards her room.

# CHAPTER TWENTY-ONE

"CHRISTOPHER, your dad is on the phone," his mom called from the kitchen.

Chris got up from the couch and removed his headphones from his ears. He was trying to lift his mood by listening to his favorite rock band on his portable cassette player. His mom did not like the lead singer's 'yelling,' as she called it, so he had to listen with his headphones when she was home. Chris placed the cassette player and headphones on the coffee table and slowly walked to the phone. He was happy to talk to his dad, but he was still feeling bad about losing Avery's journal to Riley.

"Hi Dad," Chris said into the phone.

"Hey, bud," his dad replied. "How was school today?"

"Fine."

"That's good. Have you been taking care of things around the house, like I told you?" his dad asked, sounding really hopeful. Chris wanted to make him happy.

"Yes. Mom hasn't had to tell me to take out the garbage once," Chris said, looking at his mom for confirmation. She nodded her head, even though his dad couldn't see her.

"Good job, bud! I knew you were ready to step it up

around there. Your mom still thinks of you as her little baby, but you're becoming a man, right bud?"

Just hearing his dad say those words made Chris stand up a little taller. Chris lifted his head and pushed his shoulders back. "Right."

"That's my boy! Look, I know we were supposed to hang out this weekend, but I'm not going to be able to come and get you." At those words, Chris's shoulders returned to their lowered position.

"What about next weekend?" Chris asked. "We already missed last weekend."

"I know, bud and I'm sorry. Definitely next weekend. But I know you're becoming a man now, so you don't want to spend all your time with me." His dad gave a small laugh, but Chris was quiet. "C'mon Chris. You're good, right? We'll hang out next weekend, okay?"

"Sure. Okay, Dad."

"Okay, good."

"Do you want to speak to Mom?" Chris asked.

"Um, no. You can tell her and I'll just speak with her later. Love you, bud," Chris's dad said quickly.

"Love you too, Dad." Chris said and hung up the phone.

"What time is your dad picking you up on Saturday?" his mom asked, as she stood up from the table.

"He said he's not going to be able to make it this weekend," Chris said, walking out of the kitchen and up the stairs to his room.

"What?" his mom asked Chris's back.

"He's not coming," Chris said before he turned and went into his room.

So, he wasn't going to be able to talk with his dad about what was going on - fine. He was good at figuring things out. He was also going to get good at taking care of his own problems. Like his dad said, he was becoming a man now.

# CHAPTER TWENTY-TWO

AT SCHOOL THE NEXT DAY, the notepaper with Riley's address on it felt like it was burning a whole in Natalie's pants pocket. She couldn't wait to pull it out and show that she had accomplished her mission. She was so glad when it was finally lunch time and she could finally show her prize to Skylar and Avery. Natalie had wanted to share the good news with Avery during biology, because she knew it would make Avery happy, but she wasn't sure how Skylar would feel to be left out of the good news, since they were best friends. Sometimes friendships could be tricky. So Natalie made sure to arrive to class right before the bell rang and she sat in the back of the class, so that she could be one of the first people out at the end of class. It was a great class, though. Mrs. Thompson showed a video on meiosis and Natalie was so engrossed, she actually forgot about the address in her pocket until class ended.

"So, how did it go?" Skylar asked Natalie. Her almond-shaped brown eyes were bright with excitement, as she sat down at the lunch table with Natalie.

"Well," Natalie began, looking around. Before she could

say another word, Avery hauled her leg over the bench and sat on the other side of Natalie.

"Uh uh. No you don't," Avery said. "I see you about to spill the beans before I even sit down."

"Well, you're here now and I'm dying to know," Skylar whined. "I think I missed tonight's English homework assignment 'cause I was in such a hurry to leave at the end of class and get here."

"Don't worry," Natalie said. "I'll let you know after I go. I have English 5th period."

"Thanks," Skylar beamed.

"Okay, okay. English later. What happened last night? Did you get it?" Avery loudly whispered.

A slow smile began to spread on Natalie's face and before she could say even one word, both Skylar and Avery let out a cheer. Although the sound was slightly muffled by the noises from all the other tables, it still caused Mr. Papadopoulos, the lunchroom monitor on their side of the cafeteria, to look their way for a full minute.

"Yeah! You did it," Avery cheered, trying to lower her voice.

"Dat's my girl! I knew you could do it," Skylar said, raising her hand for Natalie to give her a high-five.

Natalie eagerly hit Skylar's hand, as she beamed from their praise. It felt good to be able to help her (hopefully) new friend and make her best friend happy.

"Let's see it," Skylar encouraged, almost bouncing in her seat.

Natalie pulled the piece of notepaper from her pocket and slid her juice box over to make space, as she laid the paper on the table for Avery and Skylar to see.

"7803 Evergreen Drive," Avery read out loud. "Where's that?"

"I don't know," Natalie said, losing a little of her excitement. She was so happy to have gotten the address, she

hadn't thought about finding out how to find the house.

"I know where it is. It's in the townhouses," Skylar said, raising her index finger as if she were making a point in the air.

"Are you sure?" Avery asked.

"Yeah, Stephanie lives over there - from my scout troop. Last year when we were learning to read street maps, we had to find each other's houses using a map, to earn our badge. I was the first to earn the badge in my troop," Skylar said proudly. For a moment, her smile fell. She remembered riding her bike around, finding each girl's house in her troop. She'd been so excited when she found the last house, she'd raced home to tell her mom and had gotten all the way into the kitchen before she saw her dad's face and remembered that her mom wasn't there anymore.

"Dat's what I'm talking 'bout," Avery said, nodding her head. "Some good news. Now we just gotta go over there and get my journal."

"But how are we going to get the backpack out of the house? Riley took Chris's backpack to be mean," Natalie said, frowning at the thought of someone taking something from someone else.

"I don't care," Avery said, her voice rising in protest. "I'm going to go over there and tell him to give me my journal and if he doesn't give it to me, I'm taking it!"

"Calm down, Shirley Chisholm," Skylar said, laughing.

"Shirley who?" Natalie asked with confused laughter.

"Whateva," Avery said, rolling her eyes.

"Shirley Chisholm," Skylar said, looking at Natalie expectantly. "Don't you remember? We learned about her last year during Black History Month. The first Black woman in Congress."

"Ohhhh, yes. I remember," Natalie said, smiling at Avery. "If he won't give it back, you'll have to take what's yours."

"We'll get the journal," Skylar said, "but let's be chill about it. What if Riley doesn't know what's in the backpack? If we tell him he has your journal, then he's going to go and read it."

"I'm going to get my journal - today." Avery turned her body towards Natalie and put her hand on Natalie's shoulder. "And Nat," she said earnestly. "I really appreciate what you did. That was some real secret agent stuff you did - getting that address. Thanks."

Natalie felt her cheeks get warm, as she blushed a little from Avery's words. It wasn't secret agent stuff, it was Rachel Martinez, but they could talk about that later. "You're welcome."

"So," Skylar said, tapping her hands on the table. "We need to let Damien and Chris know, so they will be ready to go by the time we meet at the basketball court this afternoon."

"I'll tell Damien," Avery said. "We have Math together next period and he can tell Chris."

"Okay, cool," Skylar said. "Let's eat before the bell rings. I got PE next and I can't be hungry in PE."

Avery and Natalie laughed as they turned to the table to eat their lunches. The excitement of having Riley's address and thinking about how to get the journal from his house was on all three girls' minds as they ate.

# CHAPTER TWENTY-THREE

THEY ALL LEANED on the handlebars of their bikes, as they stood in a circle at the playground inside the townhouses. The housing development where they lived was very large. There were single family homes with one and two car garages on one side of the pond and townhomes and condominiums that looked like mini houses on the other side.

Damien lived on this side of the pond with his dad in one of the condos and knew the streets really well, so he was leading this part of their mission. And since his mom was in the military, he said he knew how to plan a successful recovery mission.

"I saw Chris's backpack through the window," Damien said. His chocolate brown skin was already damp with perspiration and his face looked shiny in the sunlight. He'd ridden his bike to Riley's house first, to "check everything out," as part of the recon. The girls and Chris had no real understanding of everything Damien said once he started talking in military terms, but nobody wanted to seem uncool, so they just nodded their heads and agreed, and waited at the playground until he came back.

Chris and Avery had wanted to go with him and confront Riley, but Damien said it was better to know your enemy before they know you. They were again confused by Damien's words, but Skylar thought they sounded deep and nodded her head in agreement. Chris and Avery agreed because they thought it was more military stuff Damien knew that they didn't. And Natalie's brain was frozen again, so she just blinked and stared.

"Aww, yeah," Avery said, slapping her hands together. "Let's go."

"Wait," Damien said, putting his hand on her handlebars before she could put her foot on her bike pedal.

"For what? You said it's there. Let's go get it," Avery said angrily.

"We will," Damien replied, "but we can't all go stand outside his house like a gang or something. People will notice."

"So what do you want us to do?" Chris asked. He was nervous about seeing Riley, but it felt good to have someone with him, so he didn't have to face Riley alone.

"We have to split up," Damien said. "We need somebody to knock on the front door and be a distraction, while I go around back and sneak in to grab the backpack."

"What about his parents?" Natalie asked. She couldn't participate in anything dangerous. She'd promised Rachel.

"I didn't see anybody but Riley. It was kinda weird. Like, I saw Riley walk inside, but there was hardly any furniture - like no one was living there yet," Damien responded.

"Well good," Avery said. "That will make this easier, but if you don't want people to notice us, maybe we shouldn't all ride our bikes."

"Yeah, good point," Damien agreed.

"How about this," Skylar said. "Avery and I will knock on the door and distract Riley. Natalie, you can stay here and watch our bikes." Skylar knew how easy it was for Natalie to get scared when things got real. This way, Natalie could still help and no one else would know how she felt.

"Okay, sure. I can stay here with the bikes and make sure no one takes them," Natalie eagerly agreed.

"Yeah," Chris said. "This can be our home base. Once we get the backpack, we all meet back here to make sure everybody is safe, before we ride home."

"Okay, that's the plan. Skylar and Avery will go to the door and I will go around back," Damien said.

"And me," Chris added.

"Huh," Damien asked.

"I'm going to go around back with you. It's my fault he has the backpack, so I have to do something. I can't knock on the door or he won't open it and I can't just wait here."

"But if we both go inside, it might make too much noise," Damien protested. Chris was his boy and all, but Damien had planned this as a solo mission. "Wait! I know! You can watch my six," Damien said, looking at Chris with bright brown eyes.

"Your what?" Chris asked, confused.

"My six. In the Army, when they go on missions, they always go together and watch each other's backs. The person watching always says, 'I got your six.' You can watch my six," Damien said to Chris.

"Yeah. I can do that," Chris said nodding his head. "When you go inside, I'll watch your six and let you know if anyone is coming."

"Cool," Damien said excitingly, as he held his hand up for Chris to give him a high-five. Chris hit Damien's hand and it made a loud clapping sound.

"Umm, can we go now or do you two want to hug too," Avery said, rolling her eyes.

"Yeah, yeah, let's do this," Damien said, but he and Chris couldn't stop smiling. They were too excited about doing this together. Chris wasn't feeling like a little kid today. It made him feel stronger to work with Damien and the girls to get Avery's journal, without getting help from Matt or his dad.

Avery and Skylar got off their bikes and walked them over to the empty bench at the far end of the playground. Natalie followed with her bike, and took a seat on the bench as the girls dropped their kickstands.

"Be careful, okay?" Natalie nervously said to Skylar and Avery.

"Girl, we got this. Riley is about to be missing a backpack," Skylar said with confidence.

"Or worse, if he doesn't give me my journal," Avery mumbled, as she walked back to where Chris and Damien stood. "Y'all should wait a few minutes before you go to the house, since me and Skylar are walking," Avery said to the boys.

"Okay. We'll wait until you get to the corner, then we'll ride around the back," Damien said. "Keep him busy as long as you can. It's going to take me a minute to get inside."

"This is going to be the best," Skylar said, smiling. "It's like we're all a team or something. We're going to have to think of a team name after this." She turned to Avery. "You ready Ave?"

Avery blinked. She was so surprised by Skylar shortening her name, she almost forgot what they were doing. Skylar was giving her a nickname, like she did for Damien and Natalie. Were they friends? Avery kinda felt like they were. She didn't know anyone who would go to this much trouble for someone who wasn't a friend. She hadn't expected to find a friend so soon at her new school. Then she looked at everyone on this mission with her: Damien, who was risking getting in big trouble by going into someone's house; Skylar, who was going to stand beside her and distract Riley and who'd just given her a nickname; Natalie, who'd already risked getting into trouble with her parents and come back with the address they needed; and Chris, whose fault it was that Riley had her journal in the first place, but who still came to help get it back. And who hadn't told anybody what was happening. Were these her new friends?

"What's wrong?" Skylar asked, looking at Avery.

Avery blinked again. "Um, nothing. I'm good. Let's go get my journal," she said, smiling at Skylar as she turned to walk up the path towards Riley's house.

"Let's do this," Damien said, unable to keep the smile off his lips as he looked at Chris. Chris smiled back.

"Meet y'all back here," Skylar said, as she jogged up to where Avery was walking on the path.

# CHAPTER TWENTY-FOUR

ONCE THEY GOT to the corner, Avery turned and looked at Skylar. "Hey. What are we going to do as a distraction?"

Laughing, Skylar hit the palm of her hand on her forehead. "Oh, yeah. We didn't think about that part."

"I mean, we could just knock on the door and tell him we know he has Chris's backpack, and if he doesn't give it back we're going to take it back," Avery said, with angry eyes.

"No, no no. Don't get mad. We'll save that as a last resort," Skylar said, tapping her finger on her chin and looking up at the sky, thinking.

"I've got it," Skylar said. Her eyes were large and the puffy ponytail she had at the top of her head stood up like an exclamation point. "I'll ask if his parents are home and if they want to buy cookies!"

"But we don't have any cookies," Avery protested.

"He doesn't know that," Skylar said. "And besides it doesn't matter. His parents aren't home anyway and I can say that I'm showing you how to be a scout, so you can join our troop."

"If you say so," Avery said, hunching her shoulders.

"It'll work. Just let me do the talking," Skylar said has she started walking towards Riley's house. Avery turned and followed.

# CHAPTER TWENTY-FIVE

"HOW LONG DO you think we should wait?" Chris asked. He and Damien were standing behind the fence at the end of Riley's backyard. The backyards to the townhomes were skinny and long, the opposite of the wide, short backyard at Chris's house. The fence was tall and reddish-brown, with a metal latch.

"A few minutes. I'll peek in the fence and see if I can see Riley. Maybe I can see when he gets up to open the front door," Damien said, but just as he was about to open the metal latch, he stopped and turned to Chris. "Do you know how to make a bird call?"

"Huh? Umm, I don't know," Chris replied.

"Well, we have to have a signal, so that you can let me know if somebody's coming."

"I can growl. I was the tiger in the Wizard of Oz last year for the 6th grade play," Chris said hopefully.

"Nah, that won't work. People will think it's weird if they hear a tiger in the backyard."

"What about a dog? I can bark, if I see someone coming to the house."

"Yeah, cool. Let me hear it, so I'll know it's you," Damien said, leaning forward on his handlebars toward Chris.

Chris stood tall, holding up his bike by the handlebars, and took a deep breath. "Arph, arph," he said, his blond hair swinging back and forth as his head jerked with each sound.

"Hahaha," Damien laughed. "Okay. If I hear that sound, I will definitely know it's you."

Chris smiled back and lifted his shoulders. "That's how my grandparents' dog sounds."

# CHAPTER TWENTY-SIX

SKYLAR AND AVERY walked up the cement steps to Riley's house. As they got closer to the door, they could see what Damien had meant when he'd said the house looked weird. All the other townhouses in the row had stuff on their porches to make the homes look 'welcoming,' as Avery's real estate agent mom would say. The other houses had benches and flowers or plants on their porches. Some of them even had the United States flag, or mini flags hanging with words like, 'Home Sweet Home.' Riley's porch didn't have any of that - it was completely empty and there weren't any curtains hanging in the front windows. You could see all the way into the living room from the porch. Avery and Skylar could see Riley watching a television that was sitting on top of an old brown TV stand, sitting on the only other piece of furniture in the living room - a grey loveseat sofa.

On the other side of the living room was the kitchen. You could see straight into the kitchen. There was a doorway, but no door, and a nook with a big cutout that let you see the stove, refrigerator, and kitchen table. Avery could see that in one of the chairs at the kitchen table was a blue backpack. Was that Chris's backpack? Avery couldn't remember the color of Chris's backpack, so she hoped Damien would know. And if that was Chris's backpack, where was Riley's backpack?

*Focus*, Avery thought, *let Damien worry about the backpack; Skylar and I have to make sure this distraction works.*

"Ready?" Skylar whisper-asked.

"I'm past ready," Avery said, lifting her chin and squaring her shoulders.

Skylar pushed the button for the doorbell. Through the curtain-less window, they watched Riley turn around to see who was at the door. As he stood up from the loveseat and walked to the door, his eyes were still glued to the cartoon he was watching on television.

"Remember, I got this. All you have to do is agree with me, okay?" Skylar whispered to Avery.

"Okay. As long as Damien gets that backpack. Otherwise, we're going with my plan," Avery angrily whispered back.

"What's your…" Skylar was whispering when Riley opened the door.

"Hey," Riley said, giving Skylar a singular head nod. His sandy blonde hair swayed with the motion.

"Hey, Riley. What's up?" Skylar asked, shifting her weight to her right side and placing her hand on her hip.

"Nothing. What chu doing over here?" he asked. Riley was looking over her shoulder like he expected to see someone else at the bottom of the stairs.

"I'm training," Skylar replied. "This my girl Avery," she continued and pointed her thumb in Avery's direction.

"Hey," Riley said to Avery, giving her the same head nod he gave to Skylar.

"Hey," Avery replied, shooting mental daggers at Riley with her eyes.

"Yeah, so…" Skylar said, to get Riley's attention away from Avery, before she made him suspicious. "Are your parents home? I'm, um, I'm showing Avery how to sell cookies and I think your mom bought some from me last year."

# CHAPTER TWENTY-SEVEN

DAMIEN WAS STANDING at the bottom of the steps wondering what was taking the girls so long, when he heard the doorbell. He'd done what his mom had taught him. He'd planned from the end objective and worked his way backwards. His end objective was to get Chris's backpack and now he had to go through all his steps to reach his objective.

He'd already lifted the latch on the fence and crossed the small back yard. Now, he quickly and quietly climbed the steps, up to the back porch. As he made his way to the top of the stairs, Damien had to decide where to go. Should he try to open the back door first or one of the two windows? Damien had seen enough military movies with his mom to know a mission could be won or loss by one wrong choice. He looked back at the opened fence and saw Chris nervously looking inside the gate and back out, watching for anyone who might come along.

"Come on," Damien whispered to himself, to build up his courage. "This is your mission. You can't let your team down." He had to do this for Chris and Avery. This may be his first mission with this team, but his mom had taught him everything he needed to know to get into Riley's house, grab Chris's backpack and get back to the playground safely. "Let's go," he said, as he moved across the porch. Damien decided the window would probably be the best way to go. People left windows open all the time.

When Damien reached the first window, he peaked around the ledge, checking for Riley. He saw him standing at the front door, talking to Skylar and Avery. Everything looked like it was going according to plan, so Damien looked into the house to check for the backpack.

Sitting in a chair at the kitchen table was Chris's blue REI backpack. Damien recognized the silver rock climbing clip Chris liked to keep attached to his backpack handle. Chris said his brother Matt gave it to him.

Damien tried to lift the first window. It didn't budge. Shoot, Damien thought and moved to the second window. Yes! It slid up a little, but there wasn't enough space for Damien to get through the opening. Damien moved his whole body in front of the window and pushed up with both hands. When he got the window up high enough, it made a small squeak sound - like his sneakers did on the gym floor at school when they played basketball.

# CHAPTER TWENTY-EIGHT

RILEY, Skylar and Avery heard the squeak from the back window and all looked to see where the noise came from.

"What the—" Riley said, turning his head.

"Umm, so," Skylar said a little too loud and touched Riley's arm to get his attention. "If your parents aren't home, would you mind helping us?"

"Helping how?" Riley asked, turning back around to face Skylar and Avery.

"Well, I can pretend to sell you cookies, like we're doing a play or something and you can be the customer."

"I don't know. My show is on," Riley said, beginning to turn back to the television.

As he was turning, Avery saw Damien's head coming up from the bottom of the window. "Well, just forget about it," Avery shouted and started walking towards the steps.

"Huh?" Skylar said, looking between Avery and Riley.

"Why you yelling?" Riley said, speaking at the same time as Skylar.

"If you're not going to help us..."Avery said, grabbing the handrail at the top of the porch steps with her left hand.

"He didn't say..." Skylar said, moving towards Avery and grabbing her right hand.

Once Avery felt Skylar grab her hand, she slid her right foot forward, over the edge of the first step, let the top of her body swing back, and let her bottom hit the porch, as she pretended to almost fall down the steps.

"Oww," Avery yelled, as she let go of the handrail that kept her from really falling down the steps. She released Skylar's hand and put both her hands on her bottom, showing the location of her pain.

"Hey! Be careful," Riley yelled, coming out of his front door to stand behind Avery.

"Oh my gawd! Avery, are you okay?" Skylar shouted, as she crouched down beside Avery, placing her hand on Avery's back.

"Yeah, that really hurt. Riley, I think your step is slippery," Avery said, adding a little more anger to her voice than was necessary. Her butt really did hurt, but she needed to keep Riley's TV-watching behind out of that living room a little longer.

"It is not! You just don't know how to walk," Riley said, stomping down the steps until he reached the sidewalk. "See! I walked down all of them without falling," he said, raising both his arms and pointing his hands towards the steps.

# CHAPTER TWENTY-NINE

WHEN DAMIEN SAW Riley walk out the front door, he knew he had to hurry. He climbed through the kitchen window, being very careful not to make any more noise. He crawled the short distance to the kitchen table and grabbed Chris's backpack from the chair. Once he crawled back to the window, he did a quick check behind him to make sure Riley wasn't coming back inside. Then he tossed the backpack through the open window, before climbing back out.

Damien peaked up over the window ledge again and quickly closed the window. Then he slid down to the porch floor and put his arms through the shoulder straps of Chris's backpack. Damien's heart was beating fast as he dashed across Riley's back porch. The sweat that was on his face earlier was running through the sides of his curly hair and down his cheeks. As he reached the top of the steps, he looked at the fence and saw Chris, stilling watching his six. He quickly went down the steps. When he reached the bottom, Chris stopped looking outside of the fence and saw his backpack on Damien's back. A huge smile spread across his face. His blue eyes met Damien's brown ones and no words were needed. Mission accomplished.

# CHAPTER THIRTY

AS RILEY SLAMMED his front door and went back to sitting on the loveseat to watch television, Skylar and Avery started walking back to the playground.

"Seriously. You all right, girl?" Skylar asked Avery.

"Yeah," Avery said, laughing a little, "but my butt is going to have a big bruise tomorrow."

"Sorry," Skylar said, laughing too, "but if Day got the backpack, it was worth it."

"I know. I didn't know what else to do to keep Riley from going back to watch TV."

"Girl, that was genius. I thought I was going to have to start dancing or something," Skylar said, moving her arms from side to side and shaking her shoulders like she was dancing.

Avery smiled. She was happy they were able to distract Riley, but she wouldn't celebrate until she had her journal back safely in her hands. "Come on. Let's go see if it was worth it," she said and started to run back to the playground, with Skylar on her heels.

# CHAPTER THIRTY-ONE

DAMIEN AND CHRIS were first to arrive at the playground. They came speeding down the path, almost standing on their bikes as they peddled and made a hard stop next to the bench where Natalie was sitting.

"Did you get it?" Natalie asked, jumping up from the bench.

Damien and Chris both beamed at her and Damien turned around to show her his back, with Chris's backpack on it.

"Yay," Natalie said, jumping up and down and clapping her hands, causing her curtain of hair to bounce on her shoulders and back.

"You got it," Avery said as she and Skylar reached the bench. She had been running so fast, the braids in her ponytail were still swinging, even though she was standing still.

"We did," Damien said, smiling.

"Is my journal still inside?" Avery asked, bouncing on her feet. She could hardly contain herself. She wanted her journal.

"Don't know. We didn't even look inside. We were too busy getting outta there," Damien said, as he slid the backpack off his back and handed it to Chris.

Chris unzipped the backpack and reached his hand inside.

He flipped through a couple of notebooks and loose pieces of paper. Everybody anxiously watched him, hoping.

"Here it is," Chris said, enthusiastically. He pulled the composition notebook labeled "Bio," out of his backpack and handed it to Avery.

"We did it!" Skylar shouted, while shaking her hips and doing a little dance.

"Yeah, boy," Damien shouted and threw his fist up in the air.

Natalie started clapping her hands again and bouncing up and down. Chris's face almost hurt from smiling as Avery slowly took the notebook from his hand. Avery opened the notebook and read something no one else could see. When she finished reading it, a huge smile broke out on her face and she hugged the notebook to her chest. It really was her journal.

"Thank you, thank you, thank you," Avery said, looking at Damien, Skylar, Natalie, and Chris. "I will never forget this. Damien, I owe you. And you too, Natalie. And definitely you, Sky." She was talking so fast, all of her words were jumbled and running together.

"You're welcome," Natalie said, smiling. She was so happy! She'd helped Avery get her journal back, without lying to her parents or getting in any danger.

"Don't sweat it," Damien said. "I'm just glad we got it back."

"Yeah," Skylar said, "before anyone else found it."

They all stood looking at each other. The 'not real friends,' friends. People who'd just met. The independent thinkers. They did it. They worked together and accomplished their mission.

"Well, I hate to complete a mission and run," Damien said, still smiling, "but sun's going down and I gotta get home."

"Oh, for real. Me too," Skylar said, grabbing the handlebars of her bike and pushing up her kickstand with her foot. "See y'all tomorrow."

"Yeah, of course," Avery said, following Skylar's movements, but finding it difficult to get on her bike while holding her journal in one hand.

"Avery, I'm glad we found your journal," Natalie said softly. "See you in Biology class in the morning."

"Yeah, thanks again, Nat. We couldn't have done it without you," Avery said, looking at Natalie.

Natalie was still smiling as she and Skylar rode down the path to go home.

"I can carry it in my backpack until we get home," Chris said to Avery, holding out his hand for the notebook.

Avery looked at Chris and Damien, then back to her journal. She had just gotten it back and was nervous to give it to Chris, even for a few minutes.

"Hey. If anything happens, you know we'll get it back for you," Damien said to Avery, smiling his biggest smile.

Avery laughed a little at his words and nodded her head. They had already proven that they would, so she had to trust them a little.

"Okay, but we're riding home together," she said, pointing her finger at Chris.

"Deal," Chris said, taking Avery's journal and putting it inside his backpack. He put his arms through the straps and pulled the straps extra tight - just to be sure it didn't slide off while they rode home.

"All right. Let's go," Avery said, placing both of her hands on her handlebars and her foot on her bike peddle.

"Later," Damien said as he rode his bike in the opposite direction of Chris and Avery.

"Later," Chris said as he slowly started peddling. He waited for Avery to catch up, then they quickly peddled home, trying to beat the setting sun.

# CHAPTER THIRTY-TWO

WHEN RILEY WENT BACK inside his house, he slammed the door. That's what he got for trying to help Skylar and her stupid friend. If that girl says that she hurt herself at his house, he will deny it! He did not want to give his mom anything else to worry about.

"Hey, Snuff," Riley's mom said, causing Riley to jump up. He didn't even hear her come in the house.

"Mom. You're not supposed to call me that anymore. I'm not a little kid," Riley complained, as he moved from in front of the television and walked over to her. She was holding two grocery bags. Yes, Riley thought, happy to see the groceries. Not that he didn't like instant Ramen noodles, but three nights in a row would not have been his choice. "Want me to take those into the kitchen?"

"That would be great. Thanks, Snu - I mean Rye. You're such a gentleman," his mom said as she smiled and passed him the bags.

Riley walked into the kitchen and put the bags on the table. He went to grab Chris's backpack, to put it away before his mom saw it, but it wasn't in the chair where he'd left it.

Riley quickly looked around the kitchen, as his mom walked in and put her purse down.

"What's wrong?" his mom asked. "Did you lose something?"

"Umm," Riley said as his eyes darted between the kitchen table and his mom. "No." He could have sworn he left Chris's backpack in the chair at the table.

"Okay. Well, I'm going to start dinner," his mom said as she began unpacking the groceries.

Riley looked at his mom. Her blond hair was pulled back away from her face, and it kind of had the same slump as her shoulders. She looked up from the bags and gave him a smile, but it wasn't the smile she used to have. Her eyes looked tired and the skin underneath had begun to turn dark.

"Want some help?" Riley asked.

"No thanks. I've got it. You go ahead and watch your TV show. Dinner will be ready in a little while," his mom said and patted him on his arm.

Riley walked out of the kitchen. He'd forgotten all about Chris's backpack. He was more worried about what he should do about his mom. Now that his dad was in jail and they didn't know when he was coming back home, Riley wasn't sure what he could do to help. His mom hardly ever smiled. She looked so tired all the time. And since they had to sell their old house and move into this smaller one, she hadn't even tried to fix it up. It was weird, but Riley didn't say anything. He didn't want to add to her list of worries.

Riley sat in front of the television, but he wasn't paying attention to what cartoon detective was doing on the screen. He was wondering why all of the good things in his life had changed, and why he and his mom had to suffer because of some stupid stuff his dad did.

# CHAPTER THIRTY-THREE

ONCE THEY GOT on their block, Chris kept riding past his house and stopped next door with Avery, in her driveway. He put his kickstand down and got off his bike. Avery slowly rode her bike into her garage and put it in the bike rack, next to two other bikes. Before Chris could zip up his backpack, Avery was back in the driveway, holding out her hand for her journal.

Chris passed the journal to Avery, but neither of them made a move to walk away.

"Sorry, again," Chris said, lowering his head, so the front of his hair lifted off his forehead and dangled towards the ground.

Avery took a deep breath and released it through her nose. She wanted to be angry with Chris, but she was too happy to have her journal back. She did have one question though.

"Did you read it?" Avery asked in a very small voice.

Chris's head snapped up, his blue eyes going wide. "Yes, but only the first coupla pages," he said quickly. "I swear."

Avery blinked. Her brown eyes bore into Chris's blue ones, searching for a lie, but she didn't find one. "Okay. What did you think?"

Chris stared at Avery for a long time. His mind was at war with itself. Should he tell the truth or just say what he thought was the right answer? "Let your conscience guide you," he heard his dad saying in his head. That's what a man would do. Okay, Chris thought, here goes.

"I thought," Chris swallowed, his mouth suddenly becoming dry. He squeezed the straps of his backpack for courage. "I thought, I wonder who wrote this. I wish we could be friends."

Avery looked at him, a slow grin making her lips move to the right side of her face. "Oh, yeah?"

"Yeah," Chris said, grinning back.

"Well, maybe," Avery said, walking backwards into her garage, trying to keep her face from breaking into a full smile. "You have potential, Puzzle Boy. We'll see," she said before she turned and pushed the button to lower the garage door. Chris could still see her feet, all the way until the garage door dropped to the floor. He was still smiling when he walked next door to put his bike away.

Maybe life without Matt and his dad at home wouldn't be so bad.

# CHAPTER THIRTY-FOUR

DAMIEN WALKED into his house still feeling the energy of their big win. He hadn't felt this good since his team won the little league baseball championship last season. He wished his mom was here so he could tell her how he'd helped Chris - minus the going through the window part.

"Hey, son," Damien's dad said from his favorite recliner. He was wearing his glasses and reading a book, but Damien couldn't see the title.

"Hey, dad," Damien said. The enthusiasm in Damien's voice made his dad look up from the book he was reading.

"What's got you in such a good mood?" his dad asked as he removed his glasses.

Damien blinked. What should he say? He and his dad didn't usually talk about stuff like this, but he was so happy about what they'd just accomplished. He wanted to tell someone and he couldn't call his mom.

"Umm," Damien said. Maybe he shouldn't say anything?

"Umm, what? Cat got your tongue," his dad said and chuckled.

"No."

"Then, speak up son," his dad said, looking at Damien expectantly.

Damien tried to think of something else he could share with his dad, then he remembered how brave Chris had been. Coming to tell Damien and then the girls about Avery's journal had been really brave, and Chris had done it without anyone's help. Damien had been brave with his actions; now he needed to be brave with his words. *Nothing beats a failure but a try*, his mom would say.

Damien swallowed. "I helped my friend find her notebook."

"The friend you were talking about the other night?"

His dad HAD been listening to him. Damien's eyes widened a little with surprise and he went to sit on the couch, near his dad's chair.

"Yeah, Avery. It was so cool. We came up with a plan, strategized, and accomplished our mis - I mean objective." Damien got so excited, he almost said mission. His dad used to be in the military and still worked on base. If Damien said mission instead of objective, he knew his dad would ask questions Damien didn't want to answer. An objective was a simple task to his dad; a mission involved lots of details and multiple objectives.

"Well done. I knew you were the right man for the job," his dad said, smiling.

"Thanks." Keep being brave, Damien said in his head. Today felt like a good day to talk to his dad. "I wasn't sure I could do it without Ma here to help me." Damien's heart was beating fast, as he waited for his dad's response.

His dad took a deep breath and said, "Yes. I know things are different without your mom being here, but you, young man, are very smart and capable. If you take the lessons your mother and I have tried to teach you - you can accomplish anything."

Damien blinked twice. He wasn't sure how to respond to the praise from his dad.

"I had planned on us eating leftovers for dinner tonight, but what do you say we go out for pizza to celebrate?" his dad asked, standing up and putting his book and glasses on the small table next to his chair.

"Really?" Damien asked, standing up too.

"Really," his dad said with a small smile. "Let's shake things up a bit."

# CHAPTER THIRTY-FIVE

SKYLAR ROLLED up to her house and got the best surprise! The beige Lincoln car parked in the driveway could only mean one thing…Grandma Tooshie was there!

Skylar dropped her bike in the grass of her front yard, not even bothering to put it away like she usually did. This time she wasn't looking at the bushes or the flowers. Skylar's complete focus was on the front door of her house and getting inside as fast as she could, to see her grandmother.

"Grandma!" Skylar called, as she barreled in the front door.

"In the kitchen," Grandma Tooshie called back.

Skylar moved through the living room, into the kitchen, and came to an abrupt halt. She'd been moving so fast through the house, her nose had not picked up the amazing smells coming from the kitchen, but her eyes registered the sight in front of her immediately.

Grandma Tooshie stood in front of the stove with the polka dot apron Skylar's mom used to wear when she cooked, stirring a pot with steam coming out of the top.

Skylar stood with her mouth open and tried to process all the feelings going through her body and mind. It had been so long since she'd seen someone standing at the stove wearing that apron - it made her want to cry and cheer at the same time. She wanted to cry with relief. She was relieved to have someone in the house who could help fill the hole in their lives that had been there since her mom died, but she wanted to cry because that person wasn't her mom.

She also wanted to cheer. Grandma Tooshie hadn't been to visit in a while, and Skylar had really missed her warm hugs and smiling face.

As soon as that thought came to Skylar's mind, Grandma Tooshie put her spoon on the ceramic spoon holder on the counter and turned her smiling face towards Skylar.

"There's my Cutie Patootie," Grandma Tooshie said, opening her arms to Skylar.

Skylar willingly walked into Grandma Tooshie's arms and hugged her tight. Skylar could smell the mixture of Grandma Tooshie's perfume, the peppermint candy she liked to suck on when she was driving, and the collard greens that must have been cooking in the big pot on the stove.

"Hi Grandma," Skylar said on a sigh.

"How was your day today, baby?" Grandma Tooshie asked as she rubbed small circles into Skylar's back.

Skylar pulled back so she could look her grandmother in the face and smiled. "It was awesome! My friends and I helped my girl Avery find her jour - I mean notebook."

"Aww, that's nice. I'm sure she was grateful."

"She was," Skylar said, nodding her head. "I didn't know you were coming to visit."

"Yeah, I decided to surprise y'all. Your dad sounded like he could use a little help around here," Grandma Tooshie said, looking into Skylar's eyes.

Skylar backed up and dropped her arms. "I help."

"Oh, I know you do, baby," Grandma Tooshie said, putting her hands on Skylar's shoulders. "But you shouldn't have to do so much. You supposed to be focused on school.

Now, sit down here at the table. I need me a taste tester and your dad and DJ went to the store."

A huge smile grew on Skylar's face as she waited for her grandmother to scoop some of the collards from the pot into a small bowl. Skylar loved being her grandmother's taste tester.

# CHAPTER THIRTY-SIX

AS SOON AS Natalie walked into the house, she could hear the voice of a big purple dinosaur singing on the television, and her little sisters, Isla and Luna singing along. That signaled to Natalie that it was almost dinner time. Rachel didn't allow the girls to watch much TV, but she recorded their favorite shows on the VCR and let them watch them in the evenings while she cooked dinner.

Natalie walked over to where the girls were dancing and sat on the floor in front of the couch.

"Natalie, Natalie, dance!" they chimed and grabbed her hands to pull her up off the floor. Natalie couldn't resist their cute little faces, so she stood up and started moving her hips. The girls cheered and Natalie smiled at them. They were just so adorable.

It was weird, but sometimes Natalie wished her mom were here to see Isla and Luna. Her mom would have loved to play with them and do their hair, just like she did Natalie when she was a little girl. But that was silly. If Natalie's mom were there, her dad would never have married Rachel, and Isla and Luna would never have been born. Silly, but Natalie knew that her mom would have loved Rachel and the girls just as much as Natalie did. Her mom was like that.

Just as she started to turn in a circle, Natalie caught Rachel watching them from the kitchen door, with a huge grin on her face.

"Don't stop, mija. You were doing good," Rachel said, moving her hips to mimic Natalie's previous motion.

Natalie blushed and stopped dancing.

Rachel walked over and put her hands on Natalie's shoulders. "How did it go?" Rachel said as she looked past Natalie to check on Isla and Luna. Both girls were quietly sitting on the floor, in a trance-like state, waiting for their next set of instructions from the purple dinosaur.

Natalie's face beamed. "We got it," she said.

"Oh, mija. I'm so happy for you," Rachel said, giving Natalie a hug. She leaned back and started turning Natalie around, looking at her body from head to feet.

"What are you doing?" Natalie said with a giggle.

"I'm checking for damage," Rachel said smiling. "You promised you would come back in the same condition you were in when you left the house."

Natalie stretched both her arms out to the side. "Same condition," she said, her smile matching Rachel's.

"Excelente," Rachel said. "Now, dinner is almost ready. Keep an eye on your sisters for me," she said, as she kissed Natalie on the forehead and went back into the kitchen.

Natalie sat back on the floor in front of the couch, still smiling. Just like she thought, this was turning out to be a really good year.

# BOOK CLUB QUESTIONS

1. Getting to Know You:
   • Which of the Independents do you relate to the most and why? Do you share any similarities? Do you share similarities with any of the other characters?
   • Do any of the Independents remind you of anyone you know? Do you think you could be friends with any of the Independents? If so, who and if not, why not?

2. New School Adventures:
   • What challenges do each of the Independents face as they start 7th grade?
   • Have you ever faced similar challenges? If so, how did you respond to your challenges?

3. The Power of Friendship:
   • How do the Independents work together to find the missing journal? Can you think of a time when you worked with a friend to solve a problem? What was the outcome?
   • Have you ever lost anything special to you? Did you find it? If so, how? If not, are you still looking?

4. Mystery Unraveled:
   • Were you surprised by who had the missing journal? How might you have responded if you were Chris?

• Why do you think Riley took Chris' backpack? How do you feel about someone taking something that doesn't belong to them?

5. Journaling Fun:

• If you had a journal like Avery's, what would you do to disguise it? Would you carry it around like Avery or keep it hidden like Skylar?

• Have you ever tried keeping a journal? If so, did you find it helpful to write your thoughts down? If not, how do you deal with scary thoughts and emotions?

6. Lessons Learned:

• What lessons do you think the Independents learned about friendship, trust, and teamwork throughout the story? Can you think of a similar lesson you've learned with your friends

• Have you ever had to make new friends? What advice would you have given Avery on how to make it easier for her?

7. Imagining Sequels:

• If the story were to continue, what do you think might happen next for the Independents

• Are there any new adventures you would like them to experience?

# ABOUT THE AUTHOR

Antoinette is a writer with a passion for enriching the lives of young people. Although life has taken her on many paths, none has taken her away from her love of the written word. Her love for books and the way words connect people remains unwavering. Antoinette is a city girl who now lives in the suburbs with her family.

If you'd like to connect, visit her website and sign up for updates.

antoinettehjones.com

# BONUS CONTENT

Dear Reader,

Thank you for joining our adventure! I hope you have enjoyed this part of the Independent's story. Their ability to navigate friendship and transition, and show resilience is incredibly inspiring to me. But the adventure doesn't have to end here!

Curious about Riley's life before 7th Grade? Visit my website, **antoinettehjones.com**, sign up to join the Independents family and unlock exclusive bonus material for free! Get updates, coloring pages, and more by signing up for my newsletter.

Dive deeper into the world of the Independents. Explore their stories, share your thoughts, and let's embark on new adventures together. Let's see where we'll end up next!

Visit my **website** to sign up and stay connected.

Independent thinkers unite!

Warmest wishes,
    Antoinette
    Author of *The Independents*

www.ingramcontent.com/pod-product-compliance
Lightning Source LLC
Chambersburg PA
CBHW021809130726
47987CB00010B/3081